WAYNE GI

WITH CONTRIBUTIONS FROM

MARIO RAMSAY, ALONQUIN COLLEGE, OTTAWA, ONTARIO

STUDY GUIDE TO ACCOMPANY PROFESSIONAL COOKING FOR CANADIAN CHEFS

SEVENTH EDITION

JOHN WILEY & SONS, INC.

This book is printed on acid-free paper. 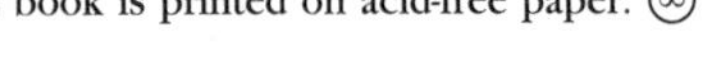

Published by John Wiley & Sons, Inc., Hoboken, New Jersey
Published simultaneously in Canada.

Library of Congress Cataloging-in-Publication Data:

ISBN: 978-0-470-60532-5

Printed in the United States of America

10 9 8 7 6 5 4 3 2

To the Student

This *Study Guide* is a companion to *Professional Cooking for Canadian Chefs,* seventh edition. Its purpose is to help you study and review the material in the text.

Learning to cook is primarily a practical, hands-on endeavor. It is, for the most part, a matter of learning manual skills by practicing them under the guidance of an instructor or supervisor, and then improving those skills by repeated practice.

These practical skills, however, depend on a large body of knowledge and understanding. You need to know about cooking theory, basic procedures, general guidelines, and ingredient information. Using this manual will help you to study and to master this material.

This *Study Guide* is arranged by chapter, corresponding to the 35 chapters in *Professional Cooking for Canadian Chefs*. Each chapter contains several exercises that you can use to test your own knowledge. Then you can see what you have learned and what you need to review. The following are guidelines for using the different kinds of exercises.

Chapter Goals

These are the same goals that appear at the beginning of each text chapter. They are not exercises, but they are included here as a reminder of the specific skills you should be learning in each chapter.

Terms

The first exercise in each chapter is a list of definitions or descriptions of terms used in the kitchen. In each of the blanks provided, write the term that is defined or described. (In Chapter 3, some of the questions in the terms section ask you to identify a picture; give the name of the item in the illustration. You will find more questions asking you to identify pictures in some other chapters.)

This is the only kind of exercise you will find in every chapter. Why is there so much emphasis on terms? It is important not only that you learn how to cook but that you can communicate with other cooks. A food service career involves teamwork and sharing of information. To communicate, you must know the language of the kitchen.

True/False Questions

For each question, draw a circle around the T if the statement is completely true. Draw a circle around the F if the statement is only partly true or is completely false.

Completion, Short-Answer Questions, and Other Written Exercises

Many exercises ask you to fill in blanks with words or phrases or to write out various kinds of answers.

If the problem is a straight question, a space is provided for you to write out the answer.

If the problem is a statement that contains one or more blanks, fill in the blanks so that the statement is true and makes a complete sentence.

If the problem asks you to write a procedure or to explain how to do a task, write out the procedure using numbered steps. You do not need to *explain* each step, the way the text sometimes does, but be sure that your procedure is complete. Don't leave out any steps.

Math Exercises

Math is very important in the professional kitchen. Throughout your career you will have to make many kinds of mathematical calculations. Some of the most basic of these are explained in *Professional Cooking for Canadian Chefs*.

In Chapter 5, you learn how to do the following kinds of math:

Handling units of measure
Working with food cost percentages
Performing yield tests
Converting recipe yields
Calculating portion costs

The last two of these are so important that you will find exercises throughout this manual to give you practice.

Other kinds of math problems are explained in Chapters 16 and 29. Whenever you have difficulty with any of the math problems, turn to the explanation in the text and review it.

Note that math exercises using units of measure appear twice, once with U.S. units and once with metric units. Complete whichever exercises your instructor asks you to do.

These are the kinds of exercises you will find most often in this manual. There are also other kinds of problems and questions that are especially included to help you review the material in a particular chapter. The instructions at the beginning of each of these sections explain how to do the problems.

Contents

STUDY GUIDE TO ACCOMPANY PROFESSIONAL COOKING FOR CANADIAN CHEFS

Chapter 1

The Food-Service Industry

This chapter gives you a general picture of modern food service and a look at the history of the profession. There is not much technical information that you have to memorize, but there are some important concepts that you should be familiar with. These questions will help you review.

After studying Chapter 1, you should be able to:

1. **Name and describe four major developments that have significantly changed the food-service industry in the twentieth century.**
2. **Identify seven major stations in a classical kitchen.**
3. **Explain how the size and type of an operation influence the organization of the modern kitchen.**
4. **Identify and describe three skill levels of food production personnel.**
5. **Identify eight behavioral characteristics that food-service workers should develop and maintain to achieve the highest standards of professionalism.**

A. Terms

Fill in each blank with the term that is defined or described.

Head chef ______ 1. The person in charge of the kitchen.

______ 2. The person responsible for preparing cold foods, such as salads, salad dressings, and cold hors d'oeuvres.

______ 3. French term for a new style of cooking, developed mainly in the 1970s, especially popular in France.

______ 4. The chef who is sometimes known as the father of twentieth-century cooking and considered the greatest chef of his age (he died in 1935).

_______________ 5. The person responsible for preparing vegetables, starches, soups, and eggs.

_______________ 6. The person responsible for preparing sauces, sautéed foods, and stews.

_______________ 7. The person who replaces other station chefs when they are absent.

_______________ 8. The French chef who is considered the greatest chef of the early nineteenth century; he refined and organized cooking, and he was also famous for creating elaborate display pieces.

_______________ 9. The person responsible for preparing roasted and braised meats.

_______________ 10. The person responsible for preparing desserts and pastries.

_______________ 11. A varied set of scientific techniques used by avant-garde chefs, including the uses of nonstandard chemical and physical processes in cooking.

_______________ 12. In a large establishment, the person who is responsible for all aspects of food production, including menu planning, purchasing, costing, and planning work schedules; in other words, the manager of a large kitchen.

_______________ 13. The person who reports to the person described in number 12, and who directly manages the kitchen production staff.

_______________ 14. The person who is in charge of the kitchen and who also works at one or more of the production stations, usually in smaller establishments.

_______________ 15. A set of techniques for cooking vacuum-packed foods at precise temperatures.

_______________ 16. A person who is in charge of one particular area of production in a kitchen.

_______________ 17. A set of attitudes and code of behavior followed by successful food-service workers.

B. Matching

Column 1 below lists some of the items prepared by the kitchen of a certain hotel. Column 2 lists the titles of the station cooks. In the blanks provided before each food item, write the letter from column 2 which corresponds to the title of the cook who prepares it.

	Column 1	Column 2
_____	**1.** Roast beef top round	**a.** Saucier
_____	**2.** White wine sauce	**b.** Entremetier
_____	**3.** Chocolate cream pie	**c.** Rotisseur
_____	**4.** Trout amandine	**d.** Garde Manger
_____	**5.** Broiled veal chops	**e.** Grillardin
_____	**6.** Waldorf salad	**f.** Poissonier
_____	**7.** Braised veal shoulder	**g.** Patissier
_____	**8.** Lamb stew	**h.** Aboyeur

_______ 9. Canapés

_______ 10. Blue cheese dressing

_______ 11. Boiled potatoes

_______ 12. Roast chicken with gravy

_______ 13. Split pea soup

_______ 14. Fried breaded shrimp

_______ 15. Beef stew

_______ 16. Chicken liver pâté

_______ 17. Baked apples

_______ 18. Sautéed veal scaloppine

_______ 19. Steamed broccoli

_______ 20. Poached halibut steaks

C. True/False

T F 1. The position of short-order cook is an entry-level job, because it requires no skills or experience.

T F 2. Institutional kitchens like school cafeterias usually do more cooking to order than restaurants do.

T F 3. Because modern technology uses so many new chemicals, food poisoning is more of a danger today than it was a hundred years ago.

T F 4. The word *chef* is a French term meaning *cook*.

T F 5. Because more and more people are beginning to appreciate fresh foods, convenience foods are becoming less important in food-service kitchens.

T F 6. Teamwork is not important in a restaurant where most dishes are cooked to order, because each cook completes his or her own specific tasks.

T F 7. Good restaurants have high menu prices, because high-quality food always costs more to prepare than poor or average food.

T F 8. The *tournant* is the cook who is responsible for preparing foods on a rotisserie.

T F 9. The organization of the kitchen staff depends in part on whether foods are mostly cooked to order or mostly prepared ahead in large quantities.

T F 10. Because of the new styles of cooking developed in the past 25 years, the old techniques of the so-called "classical cooking" are no longer used.

T F **11.** The Berkeley, California restaurant Chez Panisse, which pioneered the use of seasonal, locally grown, organic foods, was started by Alice Waters.

T F **12.** The word *restaurant* is derived from a French word meaning *fortifying* or *restorative.*

T F **13.** Modern restaurants are generally considered to have begun when a Parisian named Boulanger began selling soup.

T F **14.** The main difference between professional cooking and home cooking is that professional cooking relies on recipes for larger quantities.

T F **15.** The style of cooking called *sous vide* was developed largely by Spanish chef Ferran Adrià.

T F **16.** Training in culinary arts is good preparation for a great variety of jobs not only in food service but in other pursuits as well.

Chapter 2

Sanitation and Safety

Good sanitation and safety practices must underlie all your work as a food-service professional. The exercises in this chapter help to reinforce your understanding of sanitation and food-borne diseases, especially because sanitation is the subject of many laws and regulations governing this industry.

After studying Chapter 2, you should be able to:

1. **Describe steps to prevent food poisoning and food-borne diseases in the following areas: personal hygiene, food handling and storage techniques, cleaning and sanitizing procedures, and pest control.**
2. **Identify safe workplace habits that prevent injuries from the following: cuts, burns, operation of machinery and equipment, and lifting.**
3. **Identify safe workplace habits that minimize the likelihood of fires and falls.**

A. Terms

Fill in each blank with the term that is defined or described.

____________________ 1. A food-borne disease caused by a parasite sometimes found in undercooked pork.

____________________ 2. Any bacteria that can cause disease.

____________________ 3. Any food-borne disease caused by toxins or poisons that are produced by bacteria while they are growing in food.

____________________ 4. Any food-borne disease caused by organisms that get into the intestinal system and attack the body.

____________________ 5. Any food-borne disease caused by organisms that get into the body and produce toxins as they grow in the body.

________________ **6.** A term that describes bacteria that grow when no air is present.

________________ **7.** A term that describes bacteria that can grow with or without the presence of air.

________________ **8.** The name for the temperature range in which disease-causing bacteria will grow easily.

________________ **9.** A term that describes bacteria that need air to grow.

________________ **10.** The period of time after bacteria come in contact with a food and before they start growing and multiplying.

________________ **11.** A substance that causes an allergic reaction in people.

________________ **12.** An organism that is larger than a bacteria and that can survive only by living on or inside another organism.

________________ **13.** A general term for diseases caused by such substances as lead, cyanide, and copper.

________________ **14.** Removing visible soil.

________________ **15.** Killing disease-causing bacteria.

________________ **16.** The transfer of disease-causing bacteria to food from another food or from equipment or work surfaces.

________________ **17.** The movement of food through a food-service operation.

________________ **18.** A food safety system usually known by the initials HACCP. (Write out the five-word name.)

____

____

____

____

________________ **19.** A risk that can lead to a dangerous condition in food; a term used in the system described in number 18.

________________ **20.** An action that can be taken to eliminate or minimize a risk as described in number 19.

________________ **21.** Foods that provide a good environment for the growth of disease-causing microorganisms.

________________ **22.** Contamination of food with objects that may not be toxic but that may cause injury or discomfort.

B. Review of Food-Borne Diseases

Fill in the blanks as required.

1. *Botulism*

a. Caused by what organism? ______________________________

b. What foods might carry it? ______________________________

____

c. How can it be prevented? ______________________________

____

____

2. *Staph poisoning*

a. Caused by what organism? ______________________________

b. What foods might carry it? ______________________________

____

____

c. How can it be prevented? ______________________________

____

____

3. *Salmonella*

a. Caused by what organism? ______________________________

b. What foods might carry it? ______________________________

____

____

c. How can it be prevented? ______________________________

____

____

4. *Clostridium perfringens*

a. Where do the disease-causing bacteria come from? ______________________

____

b. What foods might carry the bacteria? ______________________

____

____

c. How can the disease be prevented? ______________________

____

____

5. *Strep infection*

a. Where do the disease-causing bacteria come from? ______________________

____

b. What foods might carry the bacteria? ______________________

____

____

c. How can the disease be prevented? ______________________

____

____

6. *Infectious hepatitis*

a. Where do the disease-causing organisms come from? ______________________

____

b. How can the disease be prevented? ______________________

____

7. *Trichinosis*

a. Where do the disease-causing organisms come from? ______

______

b. How can the disease be prevented? ______

______

8. *Escherichia coli*

a. Where do the disease-causing bacteria come from? ______

______

b. What foods might carry the bacteria? ______

______

______

c. How can the disease be prevented? ______

______

______

C. Short-Answer Questions

1. What are the three basic ways to control bacteria that cause food-borne disease? ______

______

______

2. How are most food-borne disease bacteria spread? ______

______

3. What are the two purposes of safe food storage? ______

______

______

4. Give three examples of times when food workers must wash their hands ________________________________

____

____.

5. Perishable foods must be held or stored at a temperature lower than ________________ or higher than

____.

6. What is the recommended temperature for freezer storage? ________________.

7. List the four kinds of organisms that can contaminate food and cause illness.

____

____

____

____

8. What are the four basic methods of controlling insect and rodent infestations? ________________________

____

____

____

9. What type of fire extinguisher do you need to put out a grease fire? ________________________

10. Discuss how the flow of food is considered when setting up a system for food safety. ________________

____

____

____

____

____

11. As food flows from receiving to serving, what three categories of hazards can result in the food becoming dangerous to eat? ____

____

____

12. What are the six categories of potentially hazardous foods (TCS Foods)? ____________________

____

____

____

13. List the seven steps of the HACCP system.

____

____

____

____

____

____

____

14. State the ideal storage temperatures for the following foods: Eggs __________ Raw celery __________

Whole milk __________ Whole raw fish __________ Raw chicken __________

15. Give two examples of plant toxins.

____

____

16. State the four-hour rule. ____________________________________

____

____

Chapter 3

Tools and Equipment

You might think of this chapter as a guide to the professional kitchen or as a catalog of basic equipment. The following exercises help you review your understanding of the tools you will be working with.

After studying Chapter 3, you should be able to:

Identify the do's and don'ts associated with the safe and efficient use of standard kitchen equipment; processing equipment; holding and storage equipment; measuring devices; and knives, hand tools, and small equipment.

A. Terms

For each of the first 10 questions, fill in the blank with the term that is described or defined. For questions 11 through 31, write the name of the items pictured and their most important uses in the blanks provided.

____________________________ **1.** A type of oven that uses burning wood to provide smoke or heat or both.

____________________________ **2.** Another name for a hot-water bath.

____________________________ **3.** The most widely used metal for pots and pans used in restaurants.

____________________________ **4.** An attachment for mixers and food choppers, used to cut foods into cube shapes.

____________________________ **5.** A steam-jacketed kettle that can be tilted for emptying.

____________________________ **6.** A mixer attachment used to mix and develop yeast doughs.

____________________________ **7.** A flat, smooth, metal surface on which food is cooked directly, such as pancakes, eggs, and hamburgers.

____________________________ **8.** The portion of the metal knife blade that is inside the handle.

____________________________ **9.** A sword-shaped tool used to true the edges of knives.

____________________________ **10.** An item that cooks foods by turning them on spits in front of heating elements.

11.

Name of item: ______________________

Major use: ______________________

____

12.

Name of item: Braiser

Major use: Braising stuff

____

13.

Name of item: Sauce pot

Major use: making sauce

____

14.

Name of item: Frying pan

Major use: Saute stuff

____

15. Name of item: Baking sheet

Major use: ______

16. Name of item: Roasting pan

Major use: Cooking foods.

Roasts shit.

17. Name of item: Hotel pan

Major use: Holding hot or cold foods

18. Name of item: ______

Major use: ______

?

19. Name of item: portion Scoop

Major use: Portioning food

20. Name of item: Chefs Knife

Major use: Cutting meat and

Veg Etc

21.  Name of item: Boning Knife

Major use: Deboning and Cutting meat

22. 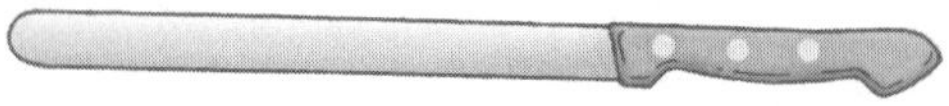 Name of item: ______

Major use: ______

23. 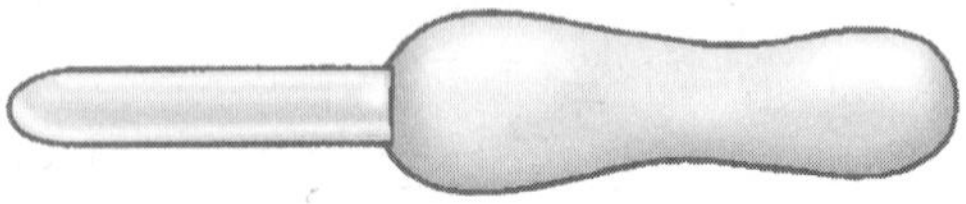 Name of item: ______

Major use: ______

24. 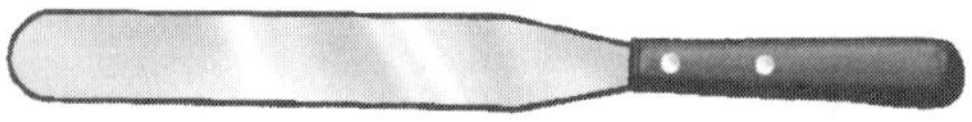 Name of item: ______

Major use: ______

25. 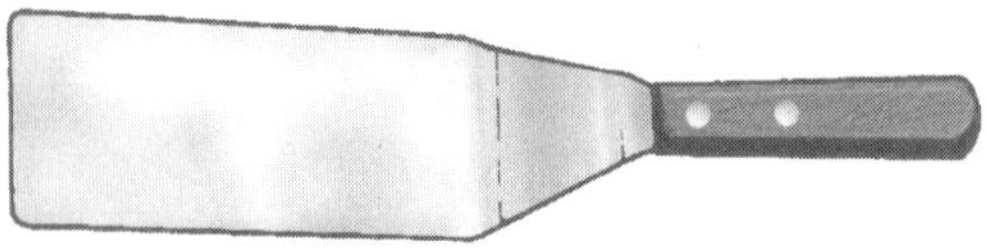 Name of item: Offset thing

Major use: ______

26. 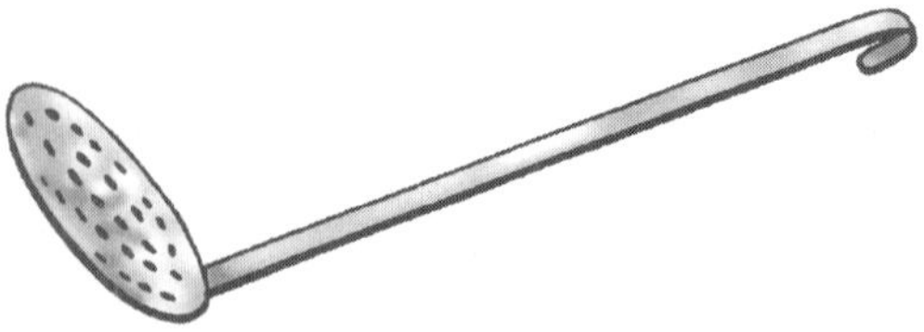 Name of item: Spider

Major use: ______

27. 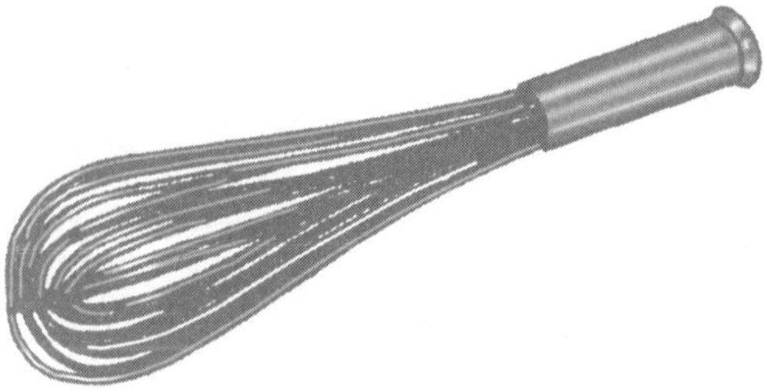 Name of item: Whisk

Major use: ______

28.

Name of item: Shienwaaa

Major use: ______________________________

____

29.

Name of item: Colinder

Major use: Straining shit

____

30.

Name of item: Ricers

Major use: ______________________________

____

31.

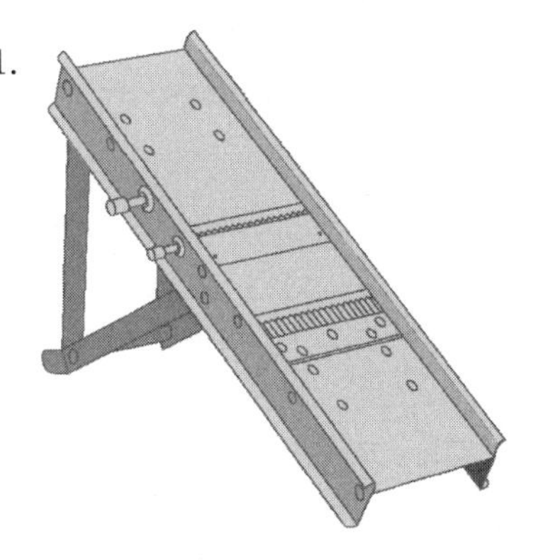

Name of item: manadalin

Major use: ______________________________

____

B. Knife Parts

In the illustration below, insert the name of each knife part in the blanks provided.

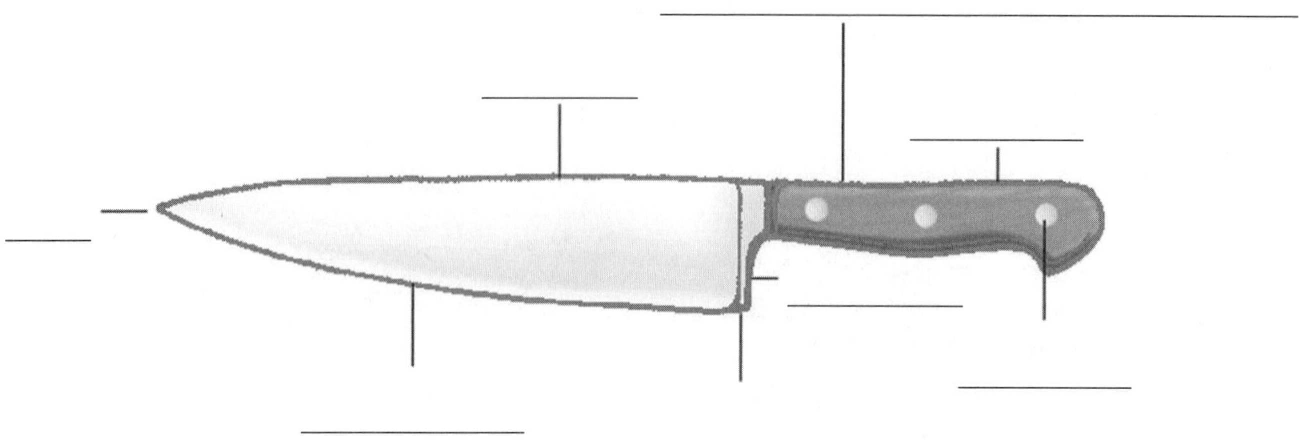

C. True/False

T F 1. If an open gas burner doesn't light on first try, it's best to wait a minute before checking the pilot light and trying again.

T F 2. When filling a fry kettle with fresh solid shortening, it is best to set the thermostat to high (375°F or 190°C) until the fat is melted.

T F 3. Because of the air circulation in a convection oven, you need to set the temperature higher than for a regular oven.

T F 4. Pressure steamers must not be opened while the equipment is in operation.

T F 5. Paddle attachments for mixers are interchangeable and can be used with any size bowl.

T F 6. Stainless steel is an ideal material for cooking pots because it conducts heat well.

T F 7. Copper is a good material for pots and pans because it is a good heat conductor, but its disadvantages are that it is heavy and expensive.

T F 8. The thickness control on a slicing machine should be set at zero when the machine is not in use.

T F 9. A Number 16 scoop holds about 2 oz (60 g) of food.

T F 10. Refrigerators operate best when they are as full as possible.

T F 11. Induction cook tops work best with heavy aluminum pots and pans.

T F 12. The temperature inside a wood-burning hearth oven is controlled by adjusting the size of the flame with the thermostat.

T F 13. An immersion blender can be used to purée a sauce directly in the sauce pot.

T F 14. A sauteuse has sloping sides and a sautoire has straight sides.

Chapter 4

Basic Principles of Cooking and Food Science

This chapter presents much of the basic cooking language that you will use nearly every day. It is important to learn these terms well so that you can communicate effectively as a professional.

After studying Chapter 4, you should be able to:

1. Name the most important components of foods and describe what happens to them when they are cooked.
2. Name and describe three ways in which heat is transferred to food in order to cook it.
3. Describe the two factors or changes in cooked foods that determine doneness.
4. List three factors that affect cooking times.
5. Explain the advantage of boiling or simmering in a covered pot. Describe three situations in which a pot should not be covered during simmering or boiling.
6. Explain how cooking temperature affects the doneness characteristics of a food item.
7. Explain the differences between moist-heat cooking methods, dry-heat cooking methods, and dry-heat cooking methods using fat.
8. Describe each basic cooking method used in the commercial kitchen.
9. Identify the five properties that determine the quality of a deep-fried product.
10. Describe the two main steps in the process of cooking sous vide.
11. List six safety guidelines for cooking sous vide.
12. Explain the difference between a seasoning and a flavoring ingredient and give examples of each.
13. Identify appropriate times for adding seasoning ingredients to the cooking process in order to achieve optimal results.
14. Identify appropriate times for adding flavoring ingredients to the cooking process in order to achieve optimal results.
15. List eleven guidelines for using herbs and spices in cooking.

A. Terms

Fill in each blank with the term that is defined or described.

____________________ 1. To cook very gently in a small quantity of water or other liquid that is hot but not actually bubbling.

____________________ 2. To partially cook by boiling.

____________________ 3. To cook covered in a small amount of liquid, after first browning the item.

____________________ 4. The transfer of heat by the movement of air, steam, or liquid.

____________________ 5. The firming and shrinking of proteins due to heat.

____________________ 6. To cook quickly, uncovered, in a small amount of fat.

____________________ 7. To cook submerged in hot fat.

____________________ 8. Wrapped in paper for cooking.

____________________ 9. The browning of sugars due to heat.

____________________ 10. To cook with radiant heat from above.

____________________ 11. The leaves of certain plants used for seasoning.

____________________ 12. The colored outer portion of citrus peel.

____________________ 13. To cook uncovered in a skillet or sauté pan without added fat.

____________________ 14. To cook with dry heat created by the burning of hardwood or by the hot coals of hardwood.

____________________ 15. To cook large cuts of meat or poultry by surrounding them with hot, dry air.

____________________ 16. Two types of radiation or radiant energy used for cooking.

____________________ 17. To cook in water or other liquid that is bubbling gently.

____________________ 18. The process by which starch granules absorb water and swell in size.

____________________ 19. The transfer of heat directly from one item to another item touching it, or from one part of an item to another.

____________________ 20. Cooking methods in which heat is transferred to food by water or steam.

____________________ 21. The temperature at which fat begins to smoke and to break down rapidly.

____________________ 22. To cook by direct contact with steam.

____________________ 23. To swirl a liquid in a cooking pan to dissolve particles of food remaining on the bottom.

____________________ 24. The taste perception of "meatiness"; sometimes called the fifth basic taste.

______________________ **25.** A mixture in which one substance, called the *dispersed phase,* is evenly distributed in another substance, called the *continuous phase.*

______________________ **26.** A mixture as described in question 25 in which the continuous phase is water.

______________________ **27.** To enhance the natural flavor of food by adding small quantities of ingredients such as salt.

______________________ **28.** To cook in a moderate amount of fat in an uncovered pan.

______________________ **29.** To cook with dry heat in the presence of smoke, such as on a rack over wood chips in a covered pan.

______________________ **30.** French term for *under vacuum.*

______________________ **31.** The reaction, caused by heat, that results in browning of the surface of meat.

______________________ **32.** The term that describes a protein that has uncoiled due to heat.

______________________ **33.** The harmony of ingredient flavors and aromas that the cook creates by selecting and combining ingredients for a dish.

B. Deep-Frying Review

1. What important quality must a fat possess in order to be good for deep-frying? ______________________

____

2. What is the normal range of temperatures for deep-frying most foods? ______________________

3. List six enemies of frying fat; for each, state one way to protect fat from it.

(1) ____

____

(2) ____

____

(3) ____

____

(4) ____

____

(5) ____

____

(6) ____

____

4. How long do deep-fried foods hold after being cooked, and what is the proper way to hold them? ____________

____

____

5. Why should frying baskets not be overloaded? ______________________________

____

6. List four characteristics that indicate good quality in fried foods. ______________________

____

____

____

C. Microwave Review

1. It is often said that microwaves cook foods from the inside out. Is this true, partly true, or false? Explain why.

____

____

____

2. Microwave ovens are probably used more for heating up cooked foods than for cooking raw foods. If this is true, why are microwave ovens so often used in restaurants where food is prepared to order?

____

____

____

3. How well do microwaves go through aluminum foil? ______________________________

____

4. Why is accurate timing important when using a microwave oven? ______________________

____

5. List three ways to help make sure that foods heat or cook evenly in a microwave oven. ____________________

6. True or false: Dry foods heat more quickly in a microwave oven than moist ones do. Explain why or why not.

D. Sous Vide Review

1. Briefly describe how tender meats and poultry are usually cooked in the sous vide process. Include temperatures and times. ____________________

2. Briefly describe how tough meats are usually cooked in the sous vide process. Include temperatures and times.

3. Briefly describe how a fish fillet might be cooked in the sous vide process. Include temperatures and times.

4. Why is sous vide cooking useful for preparing artichokes? ____________________

5. What categories of bacteria can be a hazard in sous vide cooking? Why? ________________________________

____

____

6. After cooking, foods in vacuum packs should immediately be ________________________________

or ____

7. What piece of equipment is most often used for precise temperature control when cooking sous vide items in a water bath? ________________________________

E. Herb and Spice Reference

It is important to become familiar with the appearance, aroma, and flavor of herbs and spices. Spice charts that describe flavors can be helpful, but there is no substitute for your own experience. Since everyone perceives flavors and aromas differently, a chart that describes herbs and spices in your own words can be your most helpful reference.

This chart may be completed on your own or as assigned by your instructor. Examine each herb or spice just as it is when it comes from its container. Fill in each space by describing your own impressions of its appearance (color and shape), smell, and taste. (The first column can be used to check off those spices assigned by your instructor.) The spaces at the end can be used for additional items not on the list.

√	Product	Appearance	Aroma	Taste
____	Allspice			
____	Anise seed			
____	Basil			
____	Bay leaf			
____	Caraway seed			
____	Cardamom, whole			
____	Cardamom, ground			
____	Cayenne or red pepper			

√ Product	Appearance	Aroma	Taste
_____ Celery seed, whole			
_____ Celery salt			
_____ Chili powder			
_____ Cilantro			
_____ Cinnamon, ground			
_____ Cinnamon stick			
_____ Cloves, ground			
_____ Cloves, whole			
_____ Coriander seed, whole			
_____ Cumin seed, whole			
_____ Cumin seed, ground			
_____ Curry powder			
_____ Fennel seed			
_____ Ginger, ground			
_____ Mace, ground			
_____ Marjoram			
_____ Nutmeg, ground			

√ Product	Appearance	Aroma	Taste
_____ Oregano			
_____ Paprika, Hungarian			
_____ Paprika, Spanish			
_____ Pepper, black			
_____ Pepper, white			
_____ Rosemary			
_____ Sage			
_____ Sichuan peppercorns			
_____ Star anise			
_____ Tarragon			
_____ Thyme			

Chapter 5

Menus, Recipes, and Cost Management

Chapter 5 introduces you to two of the most important documents in food service: the menu and the recipe. First, you are introduced to some of the basic concepts in menu planning. Then you become acquainted with the structure and functions of written recipes.

In order to use these documents to manage the operations of a kitchen, you learn the basic elements of kitchen math. In particular, you learn about the following:

1. **Handling units of measure.**
2. **Converting recipe yields.**
3. **Making food cost calculations.**
   (a) **Working with food cost percentages.**
   (b) **Performing yield tests.**
   (c) **Calculating portion costs.**

Exercises to give you practice with these important calculations are included here. Later chapters contain additional exercises to help you develop these essential skills.

After studying Chapter 5, you should be able to:

1. **Explain how the makeup of a menu depends on the type of meal and on the institution using it.**
2. **Describe the differences between static and cycle menus, and between à la carte and table d'hôte menus.**
3. **List in order of their usual service the courses that might appear on modern menus.**
4. **Devise balanced menus that contain an adequate variety of foods and that can be efficiently and economically prepared.**
5. **Describe the problems and limitations of written recipes and the importance of using judgment when cooking.**

6. **Discuss the structure and functions of standardized recipes.**
7. **Use and understand the recipes in this book to practice basic cooking techniques.**
8. **Measure ingredients and portions.**
9. **Use metric measurements.**
10. **Convert recipes to higher or lower yields.**
11. **Perform yield-cost analysis.**
12. **Calculate raw food costs.**

A. Terms

Fill in each blank with the term that is defined or described.

______________________ **1.** A menu on which each individual item is listed separately with its own price.

______________________ **2.** A food or group of foods served at one time or intended to be eaten at one time.

______________________ **3.** A menu that offers the same dishes every day.

______________________ **4.** A menu on which one price for the entire meal is given, and customers may choose dishes for each course offered.

______________________ **5.** A menu on which prices are listed for complete meals rather than for each separate item; prices vary depending on the meal the customer chooses.

______________________ **6.** A menu that changes every day for a certain period, after which the daily menus are repeated in the same order.

______________________ **7.** A menu that offers many courses of small portions, intended to showcase the chef's specialties.

______________________ **8.** A set of instructions describing the way a particular establishment prepares a particular dish.

______________________ **9.** A prefix in the metric system meaning "one thousand" (1000).

______________________ **10.** The basic unit of weight in the metric system, equal to about 1/30 of an ounce.

______________________ **11.** The weight of a food item as purchased, before any trimming is done.

______________________ **12.** The basic unit of volume in the metric system, equal to approximately one quart.

______________________ **13.** A prefix in the metric system meaning "one one-thousandth" (1/1000).

_______________ **14.** The raw food cost or portion cost of a menu item divided by the menu price (expressed as a percent).

_______________ **15.** The basic unit of length in the metric system, equal to a little more than a yard.

_______________ **16.** The basic unit of temperature in the metric system.

_______________ **17.** A prefix in the metric system meaning "one tenth" ($\frac{1}{10}$).

_______________ **18.** The weight of a raw food item after all nonedible or all nonservable parts have been trimmed off.

_______________ **19.** The weight of a food item as served.

_______________ **20.** A prefix in the metric system meaning "one one-hundredth" ($\frac{1}{100}$).

_______________ **21.** The total cost of all the ingredients in a recipe, divided by the number of portions served.

B. Menu Review

1. List three types of establishments likely to have a cycle menu: _______________, _______________, _______________; and two types likely to have a static menu: _______________, _______________.

2. Suppose you are planning a lunch menu for a small cafe in the heart of a business district where there are many offices and shops. What are three factors that will affect the kinds of foods you will include on the menu? Briefly explain each factor.

____

____

____

____

____

____

3. Three characteristics of foods—flavor, texture, and appearance—should be considered in order to build a menu with variety and balance (see pages 98–99 in the textbook). For each of these factors, list *three pairs* of foods that you would serve together. Try not to use any of the examples in the text. (An example is given to get you started.)

Texture Balance:

Example: breaded, fried chicken breast (crisp breading) with buttered spinach (soft).

(a) ______________________________

____

(b) ______________________________

____

(c) ______________________________

____

Flavor Balance:

(a) ______________________________

____

(b) ______________________________

____

(c) ______________________________

____

Appearance (including color and shape) Balance:

(a) ______________________________

____

(b) ______________________________

____

(c) ______________________________

____

4. From the point of view of "truth in menu," what do the following terms mean?

(a) homemade: ______

______

(b) fresh: ______

______

(c) imported: ______

______

(d) jumbo shrimp: ______

______

5. List the following courses in the order in which they would be served in a formal dinner: roast rack of lamb with spring vegetables; jellied consommé; poached fillet of sole with white wine sauce; caviar; apple tart.

______

______

______

______

______

6. The following menus are missing one or more dishes or courses. Based on what you have learned about menu balance, fill in the blanks with your own suggestions.

(a) Tomato soup

Roast prime ribs of beef

Baked potato

Vegetable: ______

(b) Cream of mushroom soup

Mixed green salad

Grilled lamb chops

Vegetable: ______

Starch: ______

(c) Shrimp cocktail

Vegetable beef soup

Main course: ______________________________

side dish(es): ______________________________

____

(d) Appetizer: ______________________________

Mixed green salad

Batter-fried shrimp

Rice pilaf

Vegetable: ______________________________

(e) First course: ______________________________

Grilled salmon steak with dill butter

Steamed rice

Vegetable: ______________________________

(f) Soup: ______________________________

Fried chicken

Biscuits

Corn

(g) Smoked salmon canapés

Beef consommé

Main course: ______________________________

Buttered asparagus

Whipped potatoes

(h) Vegetable soup

Roast pork loin with garlic and sage

Vegetable: ______________________________

Starch: ______________________________

(i) Luncheon special: macaroni and cheese

Any other course or side dish:

____

(j) Luncheon special: hot roast beef sandwich, potato chips

Any other course or side dish:

____

C. Units of Measure

Fill in the blanks by making the correct conversions. For example:

6 tbsp = __3__ fl oz
18 oz = __1__ lb __2__ oz
32 oz = __2__ lb __0__ oz

1. 2¼ lb = __________ oz

2. ½ cup = __________ fl oz

3. 57 oz = __________ lb __________ oz

4. 36 fl oz = __________ pt __________ fl oz

5. 7¾ qt = __________ fl oz

6. 15 tsp = __________ tbsp

7. 22 oz = __________ lb __________ oz

8. 256 fl oz = __________ gal

9. 12 qt = __________ gal

10. 8 lb 8 oz = __________ oz

11. 3¾ lb = __________ lb __________ oz

12. 9 cups = __________ pt

13. 44 oz = ___________ lb ___________ oz

14. 16 cups = ___________ qt

15. ¾ qt = ___________ fl oz

16. 2.6 kg = ___________ g

17. 3.5 L = ___________ mL

18. 6 dL = ___________ L

19. 1250 g = ___________ kg

20. 22 cm = ___________ mm

21. .55 kg = ___________ g

22. 6500 g = ___________ kg

23. 750 dL = ___________ L

24. 5 cL = ___________ dL

25. 4.6 kg = ___________ g

26. 550 g = ___________ kg

27. 750 mL = ___________ L

28. 50 mm = ___________ cm

29. 1.225 kg = ___________ g

30. 0.6 L = ___________ mL

D. Recipe Conversion

The following ingredients and quantities are for gazpacho, a cold vegetable soup. The recipe yields 12 portions at 6 oz each. Convert the recipe to the yields indicated.

	12 portions, 6 oz each	30 portions, 6 oz each	36 portions, 8 oz each
Tomatoes	2½ lb	________	________
Cucumbers	1 lb	________	________
Onions	8 oz	________	________
Green peppers	4 oz	________	________
Crushed garlic	½ tsp	________	________
Bread crumbs, fresh	2 oz	________	________
Cold water or tomato juice	1 pt	________	________
Red wine vinegar	3 fl oz	________	________
Olive oil	5 fl oz	________	________
Salt	to taste	________	________
Pepper	to taste	________	________
Lemon juice	3 tbsp	________	________

Recipe Conversion—Metric

The following ingredients and quantities are for gazpacho, a cold vegetable soup. The recipe yields 12 portions at 200 mL each. Convert the recipe to the yields indicated.

	12 portions, 200 mL each	30 portions, 200 mL each	36 portions, 250 mL each
Tomatoes	1250 g	________	________
Cucumbers	500 g	________	________
Onions	300 g	________	________
Green peppers	125 g	________	________
Crushed garlic	2 mL	________	________
Bread crumbs, fresh	60 g	________	________
Cold water or tomato juice	600 mL	________	________
Red wine vinegar	100 mL	________	________
Olive oil	150 mL	________	________
Salt	to taste	________	________
Pepper	to taste	________	________
Lemon juice	50 mL	________	________

E. Food Cost Percentages

For each of the following six problems, use the two figures that are given to calculate the third figure, and fill in the blank.

Food cost percentage	Portion cost	Menu price
1. 25%	________	$ 6.00
2. ________	$2.50	$10.00
3. 30%	$3.60	________
4. ________	$5.12	$12.95
5. 35%	$6.48	________
6. 28%	________	$ 7.50

F. Portion Cost

Cost out the following recipe. For prices of the ingredients, use figures supplied by your instructor or the *Sample Prices* in the Appendix of this *Study Guide*.

ITEM: **STUFFED BAKED POTATOES**

Ingredient	Recipe Quantity	AP Quantity	Price	Total Amount
Baking potatoes, 8 oz each	40	________	________	________
Butter	12 oz	________	________	________
Milk	1 pt	________	________	________
Dry bread crumbs	2 oz	________	________	________
Parmesan cheese	2 oz	________	________	________
			Total cost	________
			Number of portions	40
			Cost per portion	________

Portion Cost—Metric

Cost out the following recipe. For prices of the ingredients, use figures supplied by your instructor or the *Sample Prices* in the Appendix of this *Study Guide*.

ITEM: **STUFFED BAKED POTATOES**

Ingredient	Recipe Quantity	AP Quantity	Price	Total Amount
Baking potatoes, 225 g each	40	______	______	______
Butter	350 g	______	______	______
Milk	500 mL	______	______	______
Dry bread crumbs	50 g	______	______	______
Parmesan cheese	50 g	______	______	______
			Total cost	______
			Number of portions	40
			Cost per portion	______

G. Triming Loss

The exercises below are of two kinds, calculating yields and calculating amount needed. To do the calculations, you need to know the percentage yield for each vegetable or fruit, as listed in Chapters 16 and 21 of the text. For your convenience, the necessary percentages are repeated here.

Asparagus	55%
Apricots	94%
Bananas	70%
Broccoli	70%
Celery	75%
Cherries	82%
Figs	95%
Kiwi fruit	80%
Leeks	50%
Mangoes	75%
Okra	82%
Papayas	65%
Pineapple	50%
Potatoes	80%
Watermelon	45%
Zucchini	90%

Calculating Amount Needed

Assume you need the following quantities, EP, of the indicated fresh vegetables and fruits. Calculate the AP weight you need to get the required yield. Questions 1–10 use U.S. measures; questions 11–20 use metric measures. Answer whichever questions are assigned by your instructor. (When you have fractions of an ounce in your answer, round your answer to the next higher whole number. For example, if your answer is 13.46 ounces, round up to 14 ounces.)

	EP Weight Desired	AP Weight Needed
1. Asparagus	1 lb 4 oz	______________
2. Bananas	1½ lb	______________
3. Broccoli	5 lb	______________
4. Cherries	1 lb	______________
5. Celery	3 lb	______________
6. Figs	12 oz	______________
7. Leeks	1 lb	______________
8. Mangoes	2½ lb	______________
9. Papaya	6 oz	______________
10. Zucchini	3 lb	______________

	EP Weight Desired	AP Weight Needed
11. Asparagus	600 g	______________
12. Bananas	750 g	______________
13. Broccoli	2.5 kg	______________
14. Cherries	450 g	______________
15. Celery	1.5 kg	______________
16. Figs	350 g	______________
17. Leeks	450 g	______________
18. Mangoes	1.25 kg	______________
19. Papaya	180 g	______________
20. Zucchini	1.5 k	______________

Calculating Yield

Assume you have the following quantities, AP, of the indicated fresh vegetables and fruits. Calculate the EP weight you will have left after trimming. Questions 21–30 use U.S. measures; questions 31–40 use metric measures. Answer whichever questions are assigned by your instructor. (When you have fractions of an ounce in your answer, round your answer down to the next lower whole number. For example, if your answer is 13.46 ounces, round down to 13 ounces.)

	AP Weight	EP Weight
21. Apricots	2 lb	______
22. Broccoli	3 lb	______
23. Kiwi fruit	1½ lb	______
24. Leeks	1 lb	______
25. Okra	1 lb 4 oz	______
26. Papaya	3 lb	______
27. Pineapple	5 lb	______
28. Potatoes	8 lb	______
29. Watermelon	12 lb	______
30. Zucchini	1 lb 12 oz	______

	AP Weight	EP Weight
31. Apricots	1 kg	______
32. Broccoli	1.5 kg	______
33. Kiwi fruit	750 g	______
34. Leeks	450 g	______
35. Okra	600 g	______
36. Papaya	1.5 kg	______
37. Pineapple	2.5 kg	______
38. Potatoes	4 kg	______
39. Watermelon	6 kg	______
40. Zucchini	850 g	______

H. Raw Yield Test

Fill in the blanks in the following Yield Test form.

***ITEM:* VEAL LEG TO SCALOPPINE**

AP weight: 34 lb | Price per lb: $5.50 | Total cost: $187.00

Trim, Salvage, and Waste:

Item	Weight	Value/lb	Total value (lb × value/lb)
Fat	2 lb 12 oz	$ .05	________
Bone	3 lb 12 oz	.30	________
Ground veal	2 lb 8 oz	$5.29	________
Stew meat	3 lb	$5.79	________
Unusable trim	15 oz	0	________
Cutting loss	________	0	________

Total weight of trim, salvage, and waste: ________

Total value of trim, salvage, and waste: ________

Total yield of item (scaloppine): 20 lb 12 oz

Net cost of item: ________

Cost per lb: ________

Percentage of increase: ________

Raw Yield Test—Metric

Fill in the blanks in the following Yield Test form.

***ITEM:* VEAL LEG TO SCALOPPINE**

AP weight: 15 kg Price per lb: $12.00 Total cost: $180.00

Trim, Salvage, and Waste:

Item	Weight	Value/kg	Total value (kg × value/kg)
Fat	1.25 kg	$ .10	________
Bone	1.7 kg	.65	________
Ground veal	1.2 kg	$11.49	________
Stew meat	1.4 kg	$12.79	________
Unusable trim	400 g	0	________
Cutting loss	________	0	________

Total weight of trim, salvage, and waste: ________ Total value of trim, salvage, and waste: ________

Total yield of item (scaloppine): 5.95 kg

Net cost of item: ________

Cost per kg: ________

Percentage of increase: ________

Chapter 6

Nutrition

Chapter 6 is an introduction to the challenging and often changing study of nutrition. Here you will become familiar with many of the key terms and concepts of this science so that you can better understand how to plan and prepare nutritious, healthful meals and meal choices for your customers or clients.

After studying Chapter 6, you should be able to:

1. **List and describe the six categories of nutrients, explain their functions in the body, and name some food sources of each.**
2. **Define the term *calorie* and describe the relationship between calories and weight gain.**
3. **List and describe the eight guidelines for maintaining a healthful diet.**
4. **Describe ways that cooks can incorporate nutrition principles into their cooking and their menu construction.**

A. Terms

Fill in each blank with the term that is defined or described.

_______________ 1. A food that provides few nutrients per calorie.

_______________ 2. A measure of the relative quantity of nutrients per calorie in a food.

_______________ 3. The amount of heat needed to raise the temperature of 1 kilogram of water by 1°C.

_______________ 4. A food protein that contains all essential amino acids.

_______________ 5. Any disease that is caused by the lack of a particular vitamin.

_______________ 6. A component of some foods that cannot be digested or used by the body but that is important for the proper functioning of the intestinal tract.

_______________ 7. A group of nutrients that includes starches and sugars.

_______________ 8. Two categories of fat that are liquid at room temperature.

____

_______________ 9. A category of fat that is solid at room temperature.

_______________ 10. Of the three categories of fats listed in numbers 8 and 9, this one is considered the most healthful.

_______________ 11. Minerals that must be consumed in relatively large amounts in order to maintain body health.

_______________ 12. A type of fat that is required by the body but that must be eaten because it can't be produced by the body.

_______________ 13. A toxin produced when the body burns fat without the presence of carbohydrates.

_______________ 14. A class of fiber found inside plant cells. When eaten, it absorbs water and forms a kind of gel.

_______________ 15. A type of saturated fat that is rarely found in nature and that is usually manufactured by food companies. It is considered especially unhealthful.

_______________ 16. Combinations of fat and protein that carry fat and cholesterol through the blood stream.

_______________ 17. One of the compounds described in number 16, which helps remove cholesterol from the blood and eliminate it from the body.

_______________ 18. Two or more foods that, when eaten together, supply all the amino acids.

B. Short-Answer Questions

1. One ounce is equal to 28.35 grams. Therefore, how many calories are supplied by 1 ounce of sugar?

   ____

   1 ounce of starch: _______________

   1 ounce of fat: _______________

   1 ounce of protein: _______________

   How many calories are supplied by 25 grams of sugar?

   ____

   25 grams of starch: _______________

   25 grams of fat: _______________

   25 grams of protein: _______________

2. For each of the following nutrients, list three major food sources:

protein: ____________________

____

____

fat: ____________________

____

____

carbohydrate: ____________________

____

____

Vitamin C: ____________________

____

____

Vitamin A: ____________________

____

____

3. What is the most important function of carbohydrates in the body? ____________________

____

4. What is the most important function of proteins in the body? ____________________

____

5. Why is it important to include the B vitamins and vitamin C in the diet every day? ____________________

____

6. What is the body's major source of the mineral sodium? ____________________

Why do health experts caution us to cut back on sodium in the diet? ____________________

____

7. Give three specific examples of how you, as a restaurant chef, could reduce the fat content of foods that you prepare for your customers. ______

8. How can using the freshest, highest quality ingredients help you cook more healthful meals? ______

9. Explain the meaning of the term *empty calories.*

10. List the five primary categories of foods as described in the USDA food pyramid. How many daily servings of each category of food is recommended for a 2000 calorie-per-day diet?

11. List four types of foods that are considered to have the highest nutrient density.

12. Complete the following sentence: Considering the relationship between calorie intake, physical activity, and weight loss, the only way to lose weight is to ____

____.

13. Why are trans fats considered bad for health? ____

____

____

Chapter 7

Mise en Place

Well-planned preproduction is one of the most important elements of food service. It is essential for efficient production and service. Be sure you know this material well. In addition, be sure to practice the knife-handling techniques introduced in Chapter 7.

After studying Chapter 7, you should be able to:

1. **Define *mise en place* and explain why care must be taken in its planning.**
2. **Describe five general steps used in planning mise en place.**
3. **Explain the difference in preparation requirements for set meal service and extended meal service.**
4. **List five guidelines to observe when sharpening a chef's knife.**
5. **Demonstrate major cutting techniques required in food preparation.**
6. **Describe basic precooking and marinating procedures.**
7. **Set up and use a standard breading station.**
8. **Define *convenience foods* in the context of mise en place and list eight guidelines for their use.**

A. Terms

Fill in each blank with the term that is defined or described.

____________________ **1.** Cut into small, thin strips, about ⅛ × ⅛ × 1–2 in. (3 mm × 3 mm × 25–50 mm).

____________________ **2.** Any food that has been partially or completely prepared or processed by the manufacturer.

____________________ **3.** Cut into very fine dice, about ⅛ in. (3 mm) square.

_______________ 4. French term for pre-preparation, meaning *put in place*.

_______________ 5. A semiliquid mixture containing flour or other starch, often used to coat items to be deep fried.

_______________ 6. To cut into very thin slices.

_______________ 7. To chop into very fine pieces.

_______________ 8. To soak a food in a seasoned liquid.

_______________ 9. To cut into thin but irregular strips, either with a knife or with a coarse grater.

_______________ 10. Cut into sticks, about ¼ × ¼ × 2–2½ in. (6 mm × 6 mm × 5–6 cm).

_______________ 11. To chop coarsely.

_______________ 12. Service of a meal at which all the customers eat at one time.

_______________ 13. Service of a meal at which customers eat at different times.

_______________ 14. The preliminary processing of ingredients to the point at which they can be used in cooking.

_______________ 15. A pre-preparation technique in which an item is cooked partially and very briefly in boiling water or hot fat.

_______________ 16. The measurement of portions to ensure that the correct amount of an item is served.

_______________ 17. The basic method used to apply crumb coatings to foods before frying or sautéing.

_______________ 18. Leafy vegetables cut into thin strips or shreds.

_______________ 19. The flavorful, colored outer part of a citrus peel.

_______________ 20. Thin cuts that are square or roughly square.

_______________ 21. A diamond-shaped cut.

_______________ 22. To cut into a barrel or oval shape.

_______________ 23. Two cuts made with a ball cutter.

____

_______________ 24. A kind of marinade consisting primarily of salt and water, sometimes with added flavorings and/or sugar; usually used for meats and poultry.

B. True/False

T F 1. One disadvantage of traditional large-batch cooking for set meal service is that hot foods deteriorate in quality when they are held at serving temperature.

T F 2. For all recipes, final cooking must be started just before serving (when the waiter calls for the order) in order to produce the best quality foods.

T F 3. When foods are cooked to order, the cooks don't need to begin work until the first orders come in.

T F 4. A disadvantage of small-batch cooking is that it produces many leftovers.

T F 5. When sharpening a knife on a stone, it is important to press down firmly on the blade.

T F 6. The blade of the knife should be held at a 45-degree angle to the sharpening stone.

T F 7. Most foods hold their quality better in the refrigerator than in the steam table.

T F 8. After sharpening a knife with a steel, you should finish off the job with a few strokes on the stone to true the edge.

T F 9. The tip of the chef's knife is used for cutting small items and for delicate work, because the blade is thinnest at the tip.

T F 10. Whole spices, such as cloves and peppercorns, are more suitable for long marinations than for short ones.

T F 11. Eggs are always used in batters for deep-frying.

T F 12. Of the various types of marinades, dry marinades have the most tenderizing power.

C. Breading

In the space below, draw a diagram of a breading station.

Chapter 8

Stocks and Sauces

This is not only the first production chapter in the text, but it is also one of the most important. The techniques used in the making of stocks and sauces are the foundation of much of the work that is done in the commercial kitchen. Please study and review this material well.

After studying Chapter 8, you should be able to:

1. **Prepare basic mirepoix.**
2. **Flavor liquids using a sachet d'épices, or spice bag.**
3. **Prepare white veal or beef stocks, chicken stock, fish stock, and brown stock.**
4. **Cool and store stocks correctly.**
5. **Prepare meat, chicken, and fish glazes.**
6. **Evaluate the quality of convenience bases, and use convenience bases.**
7. **Explain the functions of sauces, and list five qualities that a sauce adds to foods.**
8. **Prepare white, blonde, and brown roux, and use them to thicken liquids.**
9. **Prepare and use *beurre manié*.**
10. **Thicken liquids with cornstarch and other starches.**
11. **Prepare and use egg yolk and cream liaison.**
12. **Finish a sauce with raw butter (*monter au beurre*).**
13. **Prepare the five leading sauces: béchamel, velouté, brown sauce or espagnole, tomato, and hollandaise.**
14. **Prepare small sauces from leading sauces.**
15. **Identify and prepare five simple butter sauces.**
16. **Prepare compound butters and list their uses.**
17. **Prepare pan gravies.**
18. **Prepare miscellaneous hot and cold sauces.**

A. Terms

Fill in each blank with the term that is defined or described.

______________________ 1. Clear, thin liquid flavored by soluble substances extracted from meat, poultry, fish, and their bones, and from vegetables and seasonings.

______________________ 2. Cheesecloth bag containing spices and herbs, used to flavor liquids.

______________________ 3. Flavorful liquid, usually thickened, used to season, flavor, and enhance other foods.

______________________ 4. Stock that is reduced until it coats the back of a spoon.

______________________ 5. The process of boiling or simmering a liquid to evaporate part of the water.

______________________ 6. The uniform mixture of two unmixable substances, usually two liquids.

______________________ 7. Mixture of raw butter and various flavoring ingredients.

______________________ 8. Basic sauce used in the production of other sauces.

______________________ 9. Finished sauce, consisting of one of the basic sauces plus flavorings and other finishing ingredients.

______________________ 10. Basic sauce consisting of thickened white stock.

______________________ 11. Basic sauce consisting primarily of cooked, thickened milk.

______________________ 12. Mixture of rough-cut or diced vegetables (usually including onion, celery, and carrot), and sometimes herbs and spices; this mixture is used for flavoring.

______________________ 13. Combination of fresh herbs, tied together, used for flavoring.

______________________ 14. Substance, extracted from connective tissue during stock making, which gives body to stock and which causes good stock to thicken or solidify when chilled.

______________________ 15. The process of raising a stock pot onto blocks in a cold-water bath, so that the cold water can circulate better and cool the stock more quickly.

______________________ 16. Unthickened juices from a roast, seasoned and served with the roast.

______________________ 17. Term used on menus to describe meats served with the juices described in number 16.

______________________ 18. Cooked mixture of equal parts flour and butter, used to thicken liquids.

______________________ 19. Uncooked mixture of equal parts flour and raw butter, used to thicken liquids.

______________________ 20. Brown stock that has been reduced until it is thick enough to coat the back of a spoon.

______________________ 21. Chicken stock that has been reduced until it is thick enough to coat the back of a spoon.

______________________ 22. Mixture of cold water and starch, such as cornstarch, used to thicken a liquid.

______________________ 23. Half onion, burnt on a flattop or in a heavy skillet; used to add color to stock.

______________________ 24. Onion pierced with a whole clove and bay leaf; used to flavor sauces and other simmered liquids.

_______________ **25.** Mixture of cream and egg yolks, used to thicken and enrich a sauce or soup.

_______________ **26.** Type of starch, used to thicken liquids, that keeps its binding or thickening power even after having been frozen.

_______________ **27.** Term meaning *until dry,* used in connection with the term defined in number 5.

_______________ **28.** Mixture of half brown sauce and half brown stock, reduced by half.

_______________ **29.** To swirl liquid in a pan to dissolve cooked particles of food remaining on the bottom.

_______________ **30.** To finish a sauce by swirling in a little raw butter until it melts and blends in.

_______________ **31.** Sauce made by thickening brown stock with cornstarch or similar starch.

_______________ **32.** Sauce made with the juices or drippings of the meat or poultry with which it is served.

_______________ **33.** Butter that is heated until it turns light brown.

_______________ **34.** Purified butterfat made by melting raw butter and removing the water and milk solids.

_______________ **35.** Sauce made by whipping a large amount of butter into a small amount of a flavorful reduction.

_______________ **36.** Purée of vegetables or fruits, used as a sauce.

_______________ **37.** Caramelized sugar dissolved in vinegar, used to flavor sauces.

_______________ **38.** Sauce consisting of a mixture of raw or cooked chopped vegetables, herbs, and occasionally fruits and frequently chiles.

_______________ **39.** Sauce based on the pan juices released during the cooking of a meat or other food. Pan gravy is one example of this type of sauce.

_______________ **40.** Mixture of chopped vegetables (and sometimes fruits), at least one of which has been pickled in vinegar or a salt solution.

_______________ **41.** Cooked fruit or vegetable condiment that is sweet, spicy, and tangy.

_______________ **42.** Sauce consisting of heavy cream that has been reduced until slightly thickened, blended with stock or other liquid and flavorings.

_______________ **43.** Term used to indicate the right coating texture for a sauce.

_______________ **44.** Stock made with bones that have already been used once in stock-making.

B. Stock-Making Review

Stock making is one of the most fundamental of all kitchen techniques, and you should be able, without hesitation, to describe in detail how to make it.

List the ingredients and the proper quantities to make 1 gal (or 4 L), first of white stock, then of brown stock. For each product, use the space after the ingredients to list the steps in production. It is not necessary to explain the steps, as the textbook does, but be sure to include all the steps, and number the steps to make the procedure easier to read.

White Stock

Ingredients: Quantities to make 1 gal (4 L)

Procedure:

Brown Stock

Ingredients: Quantities to make 1 gal (4 L)

Procedure:

C. Sauce Families I

To review the composition of the five Leading Sauces, fill in the names of the sauces, the liquid that forms the base of the sauce, and the thickening agent.

Leading Sauce	Liquid	Thickening Agent
____________	____________	____________
____________	____________	____________
____________	____________	____________
____________	____________	____________
____________	____________	____________

D. Sauce Families II

Review the composition of Small Sauces by completing the following chart. In the left column are listed a number of Small Sauces. For each one, list the Leading Sauce that it is based on, as well as the most important flavoring or finishing ingredient(s).

Small Sauce	Leading Sauce	Principal Flavoring
1. Mornay	____________	____________
2. Robert	____________	____________
3. Chasseur	____________	____________
4. Suprême	____________	____________
5. Madeira	____________	____________
6. Bercy (white)	____________	____________
7. Aurora	____________	____________
8. Bordelaise	____________	____________
9. Nantua	____________	____________
10. Mousseline	____________	____________
11. Foyot	____________	____________

12. Creole	____________	____________
13. White Wine	____________	____________
14. Allemande	____________	____________
15. Cream	____________	____________
16. Lyonnaise	____________	____________
17. Mushroom (brown)	____________	____________
18. Maltaise	____________	____________
19. Hungarian	____________	____________
20. Portugaise	____________	____________
21. Diable	____________	____________
22. Mustard	____________	____________
23. Choron	____________	____________
24. Bercy (brown)	____________	____________

E. Béchamel Review

In the following space, explain how to make Béchamel Sauce. Be sure to include all the necessary steps, and number the steps to make the procedure easier to read. Include ingredient quantities if your instructor asks you to do so.

F. Hollandaise Review

In the following space, explain how to make Hollandaise Sauce. Be sure to include all necessary steps, and number the steps to make the procedure easier to read. Include ingredient quantities if your instructor asks you to do so.

G. Recipe Conversion

The following ingredients and quantities are for a barbecue sauce recipe that yields ½ gal. Convert the recipe to the yields indicated.

	½ gal	1½ gal	1 quart
Tomato purée	1 qt	__________	__________
Water	1 pt	__________	__________
Worcestershire sauce	⅔ cup	__________	__________
Cider vinegar	½ cup	__________	__________
Vegetable oil	½ cup	__________	__________
Onion	8 oz	__________	__________
Garlic, crushed	4 tsp	__________	__________
Sugar	2 oz	__________	__________
Dry mustard	1 tbsp	__________	__________
Chili powder	2 tsp	__________	__________
Black pepper	1 tsp	__________	__________
Salt	to taste	__________	__________

Recipe Conversion—Metric

The following ingredients and quantities are for a barbecue sauce recipe that yields 2 L. Convert the recipe to the yields indicated.

	2 liters	6 liters	1 liter
Tomato purée	1 L	________	________
Water	500 mL	________	________
Worcestershire sauce	175 mL	________	________
Cider vinegar	125 mL	________	________
Vegetable oil	125 mL	________	________
Onion	250 g	________	________
Garlic, crushed	20 mL	________	________
Sugar	60 g	________	________
Dry mustard	15 mL	________	________
Chili powder	10 mL	________	________
Black pepper	5 mL	________	________
Salt	to taste	________	________

H. Portion Cost

Cost out the following recipe. For prices of the ingredients, use figures supplied by your instructor or the *Sample Prices* in the Appendix of this *Study Guide*. For the sake of this exercise, assume that the quantities given for the vegetables are AP quantities (see pages 115 and 119 in the textbook).

ITEM: **SWEET AND SOUR SAUCE**

Yield: 1 qt

Ingredient	**Recipe Quantity**	**AP Quantity**	**Price**	**Total Amount**
Chicken stock	1 qt	________	________	________
Cornstarch	1 oz	________	________	________
Sugar	8 oz	________	________	________
Soy sauce	2 oz	________	________	________
Green bell pepper	2 oz	________	________	________
Red bell pepper	2 oz	________	________	________
Onion	4 oz	________	________	________
Red wine vinegar	½ cup	________	________	________
Ginger	½ tsp (1/25 oz)	________	________	________
Salt	to taste	________	________	________
Pepper	to taste	________	________	________

Total cost ________

Number of 2-oz portions ________

Cost per portion ________

Portion Cost—Metric

Cost out the following recipe. For prices of the ingredients, use figures supplied by your instructor or the *Sample Prices* in the Appendix of this *Study Guide*. For the sake of this exercise, assume that the quantities given for the vegetables are AP quantities (see pages 115 and 119 in the textbook).

ITEM: **SWEET AND SOUR SAUCE**

Yield: 1 L

Ingredient	Recipe Quantity	AP Quantity	Price	Total Amount
Chicken stock	1 L	________	________	________
Cornstarch	25 g	________	________	________
Sugar	250 g	________	________	________
Soy sauce	75 mL	________	________	________
Green bell pepper	60 g	________	________	________
Red bell pepper	60 g	________	________	________
Onion	125 g	________	________	________
Red wine vinegar	125 mL	________	________	________
Ginger	2 mL (1 g)	________	________	________
Salt	to taste	________	________	________
Pepper	to taste	________	________	________

Total cost	________
Number of 50-mL portions	________
Cost per portion	________

Chapter 9

Soups

The procedures for some kinds of soup are fairly easy to learn, so these are some of the first products that culinary students learn. On the other hand, some other soup-making procedures are much more difficult, and require more study and practice. But whether you are learning simple procedures or complicated ones, you must pay close attention to the proper techniques in order to make quality soups.

After studying Chapter 9, you should be able to:

1. **Describe three basic categories of soups.**
2. **Identify standard appetizer and main course portion sizes for soups.**
3. **State the procedures for holding soups for service and for serving soups at the proper temperature.**
4. **Prepare clarified consommé.**
5. **Prepare vegetable soups and other clear soups.**
6. **Prepare cream soups.**
7. **Prepare purée soups.**
8. **Prepare bisques, chowders, specialty soups, and national soups.**

A. Terms

Fill in each blank with the term that is defined or described.

____________________ 1. A thickened cream soup made from shellfish.

____________________ 2. A rich, flavorful stock or broth that has been clarified to make it clear and transparent.

____________________ 3. The mixture of ingredients used to clarify a stock to make the product described in number 2.

_______________ **4.** The mixture described in number 3, after it has coagulated and floated to the surface of the stock.

_______________ **5.** A soup that is thickened by puréeing one or more of its ingredients.

_______________ **6.** A clear, seasoned stock or broth with the addition of one or more vegetables and sometimes meat or poultry products or starches.

_______________ **7.** A general French term for soup, often used to refer to a thick, hearty soup.

_______________ **8.** A soup that is thickened with roux or other thickening agent and contains milk and/or cream.

_______________ **9.** A cold soup made of puréed leeks and onions with cream.

_______________ **10.** A clarified soup, as described in number 2, flavored strongly with tomato.

_______________ **11.** A type of hearty American soup often containing seafood, potatoes, and milk.

_______________ **12.** Another name for Purée of Carrot Soup.

_______________ **13.** A specialty soup, from Russia, containing beets as a major ingredient.

_______________ **14.** A flavorful liquid made by simmering meat and vegetables, often used as a soup.

B. Consommé Review

The procedure for clarifying consommé is one that you should know well. Using numbered steps, explain how to make consommé. Be sure to include all the necessary steps. Include ingredient quantities if your instructor asks you to do so.

C. True/False

T F 1. Most vegetable soups should be cooked a long time so that the broth will develop flavor.

T F 2. The four basic ingredients used to clarify a stock are ground meat, mirepoix, tomato product, and an acid ingredient.

T F 3. When you are making chicken noodle soup, it is best to cook the noodles separately if you want to keep the broth clear.

T F 4. Beef loin is the best meat to use for clarifying stock.

T F 5. A typical appetizer-size portion of soup is 6 to 8 oz (175 to 250 mL).

T F 6. The best way to maintain the quality of a large quantity of vegetable soup is to keep it hot in a steam table throughout the service period.

T F 7. Protein coagulation is the process that makes possible the clarification of stock.

T F 8. A well-made consommé has a rich, dark brown color.

T F 9. Based on the production method, lobster bisque could be classified as a cream soup.

T F 10. When it is being clarified, a consommé should be brought to a rapid boil so that the proteins will coagulate properly.

T F 11. Consommé Printanière is garnished with various spring vegetables.

T F 12. For best flavor, it is always best to include as many different vegetables as possible in a clear vegetable soup.

T F 13. Starch thickeners help to stabilize milk and cream so that they are less likely to curdle.

T F 14. Mirepoix for cream soups should be browned lightly to develop flavor.

T F 15. A starchy product is usually one of the ingredients in a purée soup.

D. Cream Soup Review

Explain how to make Cream of Carrot Soup. Use either Method 1 or Method 2, or whichever method your instructor assigns. Write the procedure in the form of numbered steps. If your instructor asks you to do so, include ingredient quantities.

E. Recipe Conversion

The following ingredients and quantities are for a Potato Chowder recipe that yields 24 portions, 8 oz each. Convert the recipe to the yields indicated.

	24 portions, 8 oz each	**36 portions, 8 oz each**	**24 portions, 6 oz each**
Salt pork	8 oz	__________	__________
Onions	12 oz	__________	__________
Celery	3 oz	__________	__________
Flour	4 oz	__________	__________
Chicken stock	3½ qt	__________	__________
Potatoes	3 lb	__________	__________
Milk	3 pt	__________	__________
Heavy cream	1 cup	__________	__________
Chopped parsley	4 tbsp	__________	__________

Recipe Conversion—Metric

The following ingredients and quantities are for a Potato Chowder recipe that yields 24 portions, 250 mL each. Convert the recipe to the yields indicated.

	24 portions, 250 mL each	**36 portions, 250 mL each**	**24 portions, 175 mL each**
Salt pork	250 g	__________	__________
Onions	375 g	__________	__________
Celery	100 g	__________	__________
Flour	124 g	__________	__________
Chicken stock	3.5 L	__________	__________
Potatoes	1.5 kg	__________	__________
Milk	1.5 L	__________	__________
Heavy cream	250 mL	__________	__________
Chopped parsley	60 mL	__________	__________

F. Portion Cost

Cost out the following recipe. For prices of the ingredients, use figures supplied by your instructor or the *Sample Prices* in the Appendix of this *Study Guide*.

ITEM: **BORSCHT**

Ingredient	Recipe Quantity	AP Quantity	Price	Total Amount
Beef brisket	2 lb	______	______	______
Beef stock	3½ qt	______	______	______
Butter	4 oz	______	______	______
Onion, EP*	8 oz	______	______	______
Leeks, EP*	8 oz	______	______	______
Cabbage, EP*	8 oz	______	______	______
Beets	2 No. 2½ cans	______	______	______
Tomato purée	4 oz	______	______	______
Red wine vinegar	4 oz	______	______	______
Sugar	1 oz	______	______	______
Sour cream	12 oz	______	______	______
			Total cost	______
			Number of portions	24
			Cost per portion	______

**Note:* Remember that you need AP weights of all ingredients (see pages 115 and 119 in the textbook). Let's assume that you kept a record of the quantities needed when you made this recipe:

To get 8 oz EP onions, you needed 9 oz AP.
To get 8 oz EP leeks, you needed 1 lb AP.
To get 8 oz EP cabbage, you needed 10 oz AP.

Portion Cost—Metric

Cost out the following recipe. For prices of the ingredients, either use figures supplied by your instructor, or use the *Sample Prices* in the Appendix of this *Study Guide*.

ITEM: **BORSCHT**

Ingredient	Recipe Quantity	AP Quantity	Price	Total Amount
Beef brisket	1 kg	________	________	________
Beef stock	3.5 L	________	________	________
Butter	100 g	________	________	________
Onion, EP*	250 g	________	________	________
Leeks, EP*	250 g	________	________	________
Cabbage, EP*	250 g	________	________	________
Beets	2 No. 2½ cans	________	________	________
Tomato purée	125 g	________	________	________
Red wine vinegar	125 mL	________	________	________
Sugar	25 g	________	________	________
Sour cream	400 g	________	________	________
			Total cost	________
			Number of portions	24
			Cost per portion	________

**Note:* Remember that you need AP weights of all ingredients (see pages 115 and 119 in the textbook). Let's assume that you kept a record of the quantities needed when you made this recipe:

To get 250 g EP onions, you needed 275 g AP.
To get 250 g EP leeks, you needed 500 g AP.
To get 250 g EP cabbage, you needed 300 g AP.

Chapter 10

Understanding Meats and Game

Meats are such a large area of study that we have divided the subject matter into two chapters. This first chapter concentrates on basic product information. In particular, it discusses the general characteristics of the four most important meats—beef, lamb, veal, and pork. The great variety of meat cuts may be somewhat confusing at first, so careful review is called for.

After studying Chapter 10, you should be able to:

1. **Describe the composition and structure of meat and explain how they relate to meat selection and cooking methods.**
2. **Explain the use of the federal meat inspection and grading system in selecting and purchasing meats.**
3. **Explain the effect that aging has on meat and identify the two primary aging methods.**
4. **Identify the primal cuts of beef, lamb, veal, and pork, and list the major fabricated cuts obtained from each of them.**
5. **Select appropriate cooking methods for the most important meat cuts, based on the meat's tenderness and other characteristics.**
6. **Prepare variety meats.**
7. **Identify the characteristics of game meats and select the appropriate cooking methods for them.**
8. **Determine doneness in cooked meats.**
9. **Store fresh meats and frozen meat to gain the maximum shelf life.**

A. Terms

Fill in each blank with the term that is defined or described.

______________________ 1. In a piece of meat, the fat that is deposited within the muscle tissue.

______________________ 2. A type of connective tissue in meats that dissolves when cooked with moisture.

______________________ 3. A type of connective tissue that does not break down or dissolve when cooked.

______________________ **4.** A government procedure that checks the wholesomeness of meat, to make sure that it is fit to eat.

______________________ **5.** A government procedure that checks the quality of meat.

______________________ **6.** Meat that has not had enough time after slaughter to develop tenderness and flavor.

______________________ **7.** One of the primary divisions of meat quarters, foresaddles, hindsaddles, and carcasses as they are broken down into smaller cuts.

______________________ **8.** The continued rise of a roast's internal temperature after it has been removed from the oven.

______________________ **9.** The name given to the degree of doneness of a piece of meat that is cooked on the outside but still uncooked or barely cooked on the inside.

______________________ **10.** A disease that could be transmitted by eating undercooked pork.

______________________ **11.** The four-word term that the letters IMPS stand for.

____

____

____

______________________ **12.** A grading system that indicates how much usable meat a carcass has in proportion to fat.

______________________ **13.** The process of inserting strips of fat into a piece of meat, usually a cut of meat that has little of its own fat.

______________________ **14.** The process of tying sheets of fat over the surface of a cut of meat that does not have its own natural fat cover.

______________________ **15.** A group of meats consisting of organs, glands, and other meats that don't form part of the dressed carcass of the animal.

______________________ **16.** The thymus gland of calves and other young animals, used as food.

______________________ **17.** The muscular stomach lining of the beef animal, used as food.

______________________ **18.** Pork intestines, used as food.

______________________ **19.** A fatty membrane covering a pig's stomach.

______________________ **20.** Deer meat.

______________________ **21.** Wild pig.

______________________ **22.** An animal similar to rabbit but with dark red, gamy meat.

______________________ **23.** The process of exposing foods to radiation in order to kill bacteria, parasites, and other potentially harmful organisms.

______________________ **24.** The process of holding dressed carcasses of game animals or birds outside of refrigeration for a period before further cutting, processing, or cooking.

B. Short-Answer Questions

Fill in the blanks to complete the following statements. You may need more than one word per blank.

1. The most accurate way to test the doneness of a roast is to ____________________.

2. As meat is aged, it gradually becomes tenderer. This is caused by ____________________, which are naturally present in the meat.

3. ____________________ is not aged because it doesn't have enough fat cover to protect it from drying out.

4. A meat is naturally tender if it comes from a ____________________ animal or if it comes from a muscle that had ____________________ exercise.

5. Quality grading of meats ____________________ (is/is not) required by law.

6. Some connective tissues can be broken down by heat, by acids, or by ____________________.

7. The top grade of beef is ____________________. The next two grades, in order, are ____________________ and ____________________.

8. The top three grades of veal, starting with the best, are ____________________, ____________________, and ____________________.

9. The top three grades of lamb, starting with the best, are ____________________, ____________________, and ____________________.

10. The first cut made to break down a carcass of veal is located between ____________________ ____________________. This divides the carcass into two pieces called the ____________________ ____________________ and the ____________________.

11. The first cut made to break down a carcass of beef is to divide it into two halves, called ____________________, by cutting it ____________________.

12. The major bones in a primal rib of beef are ____________________ ____________________.

13. The bone that forms the stem of the T in a T-bone steak is called the ____________________.

14. The major bones in a full loin of beef are ______________________________

______________________________.

15. The full loin of beef may be divided into two parts, called the ______________ and the ______________.

16. The standard full rack of lamb contains how many ribs? ______________

17. The major bones in a primal leg of veal are ______________________________

______________________________.

18. Two examples of beef cuts that are almost always cooked by moist-heat methods are ______________

and ______________.

19. Two examples of beef cuts that are almost always cooked by dry-heat methods are ______________

and ______________.

20. The usual method used to test the doneness of a steak being cooked on a grill is ______________.

21. Of the four types of kidneys discussed, ______________ kidneys and ______________ kidneys are considered the most desirable.

22. The best way to cook tripe is by ______________.

23. Tender cuts of venison, such as the loin, are best cooked to the rare stage because ______________

______________________________.

24. The common meat that bison or buffalo most resembles is ______________.

25. The most desirable parts of the rabbit carcass are the ______________ and the ______________.

C. Beef Primal Cuts

Cuts are identified by numbers in the following beef chart. In each of the numbered blanks after the chart, write the name of the cut corresponding to the number in the chart.

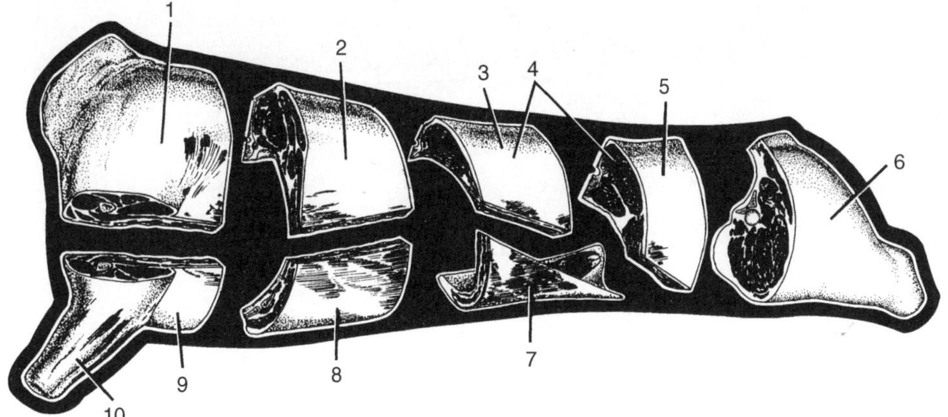

1. ______________________
2. ______________________
3. ______________________
4. ______________________
5. ______________________
6. ______________________
7. ______________________
8. ______________________
9. ______________________
10. ______________________

D. Pork Cuts

Cuts are identified by numbers in the following pork chart. In each of the numbered blanks after the chart, write the name of the cut corresponding to the number in the chart.

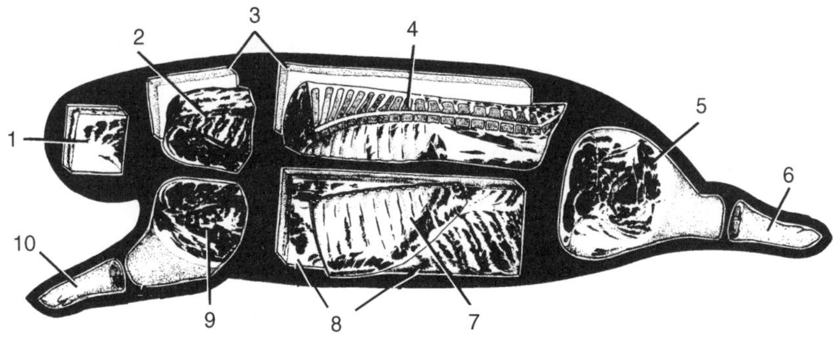

1. ______________________
2. ______________________
3. ______________________
4. ______________________
5. ______________________
6. ______________________
7. ______________________
8. ______________________
9. ______________________
10. ______________________

E. The Round or Leg

Identify the various parts in the following diagram of a round steak, and fill in the numbered blanks with the names of the parts.

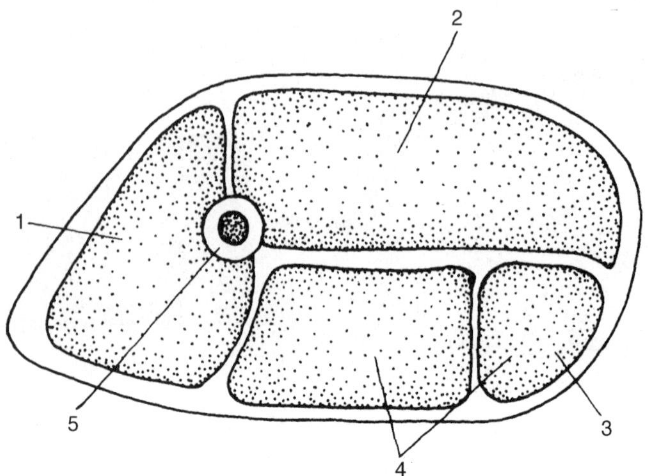

1. ______________________

2. ______________________

3. ______________________

4. ______________________

5. ______________________

F. Fabricated Cuts

In the blank following the name of each cut, write the name of the primal cut from which it is taken.

1. Beef shoulder clod ______________________

2. Lamb rib chop ______________________

3. Beef sirloin steak ______________________

4. Veal loin chop ______________________

5. Beef rump ______________________

6. Canadian-style bacon ______________________

7. Boneless lamb rolled shoulder roast ____________________
8. Corned beef brisket ____________________
9. Beef porterhouse steak ____________________
10. Beef flank steak ____________________
11. Pork rib chop ____________________
12. Beef knuckle ____________________
13. Beef hamburger ____________________
14. Smoked daisy ham ____________________
15. Bacon ____________________
16. Leg of lamb roast ____________________
17. Veal scaloppine ____________________
18. Beef tenderloin steak ____________________
19. Beef short ribs ____________________
20. Beef top round ____________________
21. Smoked picnic ham ____________________
22. Veal saddle roast ____________________
23. Beef T-bone steak ____________________
24. Beef strip loin steak ____________________
25. Lamb sirloin chop ____________________

G. Raw Yield Test

Fill in the blanks in the following Yield Test form. (Instructions for completing this form are in Chapter 5 of the textbook, pages 109–110.)

ITEM: **BEEF STRIP LOIN (BONE IN) REGULAR TO TRIMMED STRIP LOIN STEAKS**

AP weight: 18 lb | Price per lb: $2.99 | Total cost: $53.82

Trim, Salvage, and Waste:

Item	Weight	Value/lb	Total value (lb × value/lb)
Fat	2 lb 9 oz	$ .07	________
Bone	4 lb 2 oz	.24	________
Ground beef	11 oz	$2.39	________
Cutting loss	________	0	________

Total weight of trim, salvage, and waste:	________	Total value of trim, salvage, and waste:	________
Total yield of item (steaks):	10 lb 8 oz		
Net cost of item:	________		
Cost per lb:	________		
Percentage of increase:	________		

Raw Yield Test—Metric

Fill in the blanks in the following Yield Test form. (Instructions for completing this form are in Chapter 5 of the textbook, pages 109-110, and in Appendix 4, page 1029.)

***ITEM:* BEEF STRIP LOIN (BONE IN) REGULAR TO TRIMMED STRIP LOIN STEAKS**

AP weight: 8 kg Price per kg: $6.79 Total cost: $54.32

Trim, Salvage, and Waste:

Item	Weight	Value/kg	Total value (kg × value/kg)
Fat	1.2 kg	$ .15	______
Bone	1.9 kg	.55	______
Ground beef	350 g	$5.25	______
Cutting loss	______	0	______

Total weight of trim, salvage, and waste: ______ Total value of trim, salvage, and waste: ______

Total yield of item (steaks): 4.5 kg

Net cost of item: ______

Cost per kg: ______

Percentage of increase: ______

Chapter 11

Cooking Meats and Game

In this chapter, our examination shifts from product information to cooking techniques. The basic cooking methods, first discussed in Chapter 4, are applied to a range of meat types and cuts.

After studying Chapter 11, you should be able to:

1. **Cook meats by roasting and baking.**
2. **Cook meats by broiling, grilling, and pan-broiling.**
3. **Cook meats by sautéing, pan-frying, and griddling.**
4. **Cook meats by simmering.**
5. **Cook meats by braising.**
6. **Cook variety meats.**

A. Terms

Fill in each blank with the term that is defined or described.

____________________ **1.** Spooning fat drippings over a roast as it cooks.

____________________ **2.** To cook foods by surrounding them with hot, dry air.

____________________ **3.** Meat juice thickened with cornstarch or similar starch, served as a sauce with the meat.

____________________ **4.** A mixture of chopped parsley, bread crumbs, and garlic, used as a coating or topping for items such as roast rack of lamb.

_______________ **5.** The process of stripping all the meat and fat off the ends of the rib bones on a roast, especially rack of lamb, for the sake of appearance.

_______________ **6.** A German dish consisting of beef marinated and then cooked with vinegar and other ingredients.

_______________ **7.** A brown lamb stew.

_______________ **8.** To place meats on a grill or broiler in such a way that the hot bars of the grill make an attractive cross-hatching pattern on the meat.

_______________ **9.** A broiled dish consisting of cubes of meat, usually lamb, and sometimes vegetables threaded on skewers.

_______________ **10.** The muscular stomach lining of the beef animal, used as food.

_______________ **11.** Thin, flattened slices of veal leg, usually cooked by sautéing.

_______________ **12.** Flank steak or other cut of beef broiled rare and cut in thin slices.

_______________ **13.** Beef round steaks braised in brown sauce.

_______________ **14.** A small beef tenderloin steak cut about 1½ in. (4 cm) thick and weighing about 3 oz (90 g).

_______________ **15.** A dish consisting of sautéed beef tenderloin tips in a sauce made with sour cream.

_______________ **16.** To cook small pieces of meat by simmering or braising in a small amount of liquid that is then served with the meat as a sauce.

_______________ **17.** A dish consisting of simmered corned beef and simmered vegetables, served together.

_______________ **18.** A white stew of white meats cooked by simmering without preliminary browning, and served with a white sauce.

_______________ **19.** A white stew made by cooking white meat in fat over low heat, without letting it brown, and then cooking in liquid.

_______________ **20.** A common name for a large cut of meat, usually beef, cooked by braising.

_______________ **21.** A classic French beef stew cooked in red wine and garnished with bacon pieces, mushrooms, and small onions.

_______________ **22.** A Hungarian stew flavored with paprika.

_______________ **23.** To swirl a liquid in a sauté pan or other pan to dissolve cooked particles of food remaining on the bottom.

_______________ **24.** A North African spiced stew, traditionally cooked in an earthenware pot with a conical lid.

B. Roasting Review

The following statements consist of instructions and guidelines for roasting meats, but some key words are left out. Fill in the blanks to complete the sentences.

1. Select a roasting pan that has ____________ sides; the size of the pan should be ____________ ____________.

2. When you are trimming the meat for a roast, heavy fat coverings should be ____________ ____________.

3. Unless it is a bone-in rib roast, the meat should be placed on a ____________.

4. The fat side of the meat should be ____________ when it is placed in the pan.

5. If you are using a standard meat thermometer instead of an instant-read thermometer, position it in the meat so that the tip is ____________.

6. The oven should be ____________ before the roast is put in.

7. If you are using a convection oven in place of a conventional oven, set the temperature ____________.

8. Most large roasts cook best at a ____________ temperature.

9. Do not put a ____________ on the pan, because this will trap ____________ in the pan. Roasting is supposed to be a dry-heat cooking method.

10. The main purpose of using mirepoix when roasting meats is ____________ ____________.

11. Because of carry-over cooking, the meat should be removed from the oven ____________.

12. After the roast is removed from the oven, allow it to ____________ ____________.

13. If the cooked roast must be held in a warmer for a relatively long time, set the temperature ____________ ____________.

C. Braising Review

In one method for braising meats, the meat is cooked in a thickened sauce. Below are the steps for this procedure, but they are all out of order. Place the steps in the correct order by writing the number 1 in the blank before the first step, number 2 before the second step, and so on.

Caution: The steps may not all be written in the same way as in the text. In some cases, one step in the text may be divided into two steps here. In other cases, two steps might be combined into one step here. So think about the methods, and don't just copy the book.

_______ Add flour to make a roux.

_______ Adjust the seasonings and thickness of the sauce and skim off excess fat as necessary before serving.

_______ Heat a small amount of fat in the braising pan.

_______ Simmer with the cover on until the meat is tender.

_______ Collect all equipment and food supplies.

_______ Brown the roux.

_______ Put the meat in the pan and brown it well on all sides. Remove it from the pan.

_______ Return the meat to the pan.

_______ Stir in the stock and simmer until thickened.

_______ Add the mirepoix and brown it in the fat left in the pan.

_______ Add tomato product and sachet.

_______ Trim and prepare the meat for cooking as required.

In another method for braising meats, the meat is cooked in a flavorful stock instead of a thickened sauce, and braising liquid is made into a sauce after the meat is cooked. Below are the steps for this procedure, again out of order. Put them in the right order as in the above exercise.

_______ Skim the fat from the braising liquid. Make a roux and thicken the braising liquid with it to make a sauce.

_______ Add the mirepoix and brown it in the fat left in the pan.

_______ Strain and adjust the seasonings of the sauce.

_______ Collect all equipment and food supplies.

_______ Put the meat in the pan and brown it well on all sides. Remove it from the pan.

_______ Serve the meat with the sauce.

_______ Heat a small amount of fat in the braising pan.

_______ Put the meat back into the pan and add stock or other braising liquids, plus tomato product and sachet.

_______ Trim and prepare the meat for cooking as required.

_______ Take the cooked meat out of the braising liquid and keep the meat warm.

_______ Simmer with the cover on until the meat is tender.

D. True/False

T F 1. If you are broiling two 1-inch-thick steaks, and one of them has been ordered well done while the other is to be rare, you should cook the well-done steak over higher heat.

T F 2. Veal leg and veal shank are two good cuts to use for veal scaloppine.

T F 3. Rack of lamb to be done rare should always be roasted at a low temperature.

T F 4. Lamb shoulder is a suitable cut to be cooked by braising.

T F 5. When sautéeing beef tenderloin tips, you should make sure the pan is hot before you add the meat.

T F 6. Since oxtails are not naturally tender, they should be cooked by simmering or braising.

T F 7. Salted and cured meats to be simmered are generally started in cold water.

T F 8. A rule of thumb for broiling meats is "The shorter the cooking time, the higher the cooking temperature."

T F 9. To sauté meats in the most efficient way, you should make sure that you use a small enough pan so that the meat covers the bottom completely.

T F 10. Clarified butter should never be used for sautéing.

T F 11. For some sautéed meat recipes, the pan that the meat was cooked in is deglazed to make a sauce for the meat.

T F 12. When simmering corned beef, you should use enough cooking liquid to cover the meat by about one-third.

T F 13. Stir-frying is similar to sautéing, except that in stir-frying, food items are mixed by flipping the pan, while in sautéing they are turned over with a spatula.

E. Recipe Conversion

The following ingredients and quantities are for a Roast Stuffed Lamb Shoulder recipe that yields 10 portions, 5 oz each. Convert the recipe to the yields indicated.

	10 portions, 5 oz each	30 portions, 5 oz each	75 portions, 4 oz each
Onion	4 oz	______	______
Garlic	1 tsp	______	______
Oil	2 oz	______	______
Bread crumbs, fresh	3 oz	______	______
Chopped parsley	⅓ cup	______	______
Rosemary	½ tsp	______	______
Black pepper	¼ tsp	______	______
Salt	½ tsp	______	______
Eggs, beaten	1	______	______
Boneless lamb shoulder	4 lb	______	______
Mirepoix	8 oz	______	______
Flour	2 oz	______	______
Brown stock	1 qt	______	______
Tomatoes, canned	4 oz	______	______

Recipe Conversion—Metric

The following ingredients and quantities are for a Roast Stuffed Lamb Shoulder recipe that yields 10 portions, 150 g each. Convert the recipe to the yields indicated.

	10 portions, 150 g each	**30 portions, 150 g each**	**75 portions, 125 g each**
Onion	125 g	______	______
Garlic	5 mL	______	______
Oil	50 mL	______	______
Bread crumbs, fresh	100 g	______	______
Chopped parsley	75 mL	______	______
Rosemary	2 mL	______	______
Black pepper	1 mL	______	______
Salt	2 mL	______	______
Eggs, beaten	1	______	______
Boneless lamb shoulder	2 kg	______	______
Mirepoix	250 g	______	______
Flour	50 g	______	______
Brown stock	1 L	______	______
Tomatoes, canned	125 g	______	______

F. Portion Cost

Cost out the following recipe. For prices of the ingredients, use figures supplied by your instructor or the *Sample Prices* in the Appendix of this *Study Guide*.

***ITEM:* CHILE CON CARNE**

Ingredient	Recipe Quantity	AP Quantity	Price	Total Amount
Onion, EP*	2½ lb	________	________	________
Green pepper, EP*	1¼ lb	________	________	________
Vegetable oil	4 oz	________	________	________
Ground beef	5 lb	________	________	________
Tomatoes	#10 can	________	________	________
Tomato paste	10 oz	________	________	________
Beef stock	2½ pt	________	________	________
Chili powder	3 oz	________	________	________
			Total cost	________
			Number of portions	24
			Cost per portion	________

**Note:* Remember that you need AP weights of all ingredients (see pages 115 and 119 in the text). Let's assume that you kept a record of the quantities needed when you made this recipe:

To get 2½ lb EP onions, you needed 2 lb 12 oz AP.
To get 1¼ lb EP green pepper, you needed 1½ lb AP.

Portion Cost—Metric

Cost out the following recipe. For prices of the ingredients, use figures supplied by your instructor or the *Sample Prices* in the Appendix of this *Study Guide*.

ITEM: **CHILE CON CARNE**

Ingredient	Recipe Quantity	AP Quantity	Price	Total Amount
Onion, EP*	1.25 kg	______	______	______
Green pepper, EP*	600 g	______	______	______
Vegetable oil	125 mL	______	______	______
Ground beef	2.5 kg	______	______	______
Tomatoes	#10 can	______	______	______
Tomato paste	300 g	______	______	______
Beef stock	1.25 L	______	______	______
Chili powder	100 g	______	______	______
			Total cost	______
			Number of portions	24
			Cost per portion	______

**Note:* Remember that you need AP weights of all ingredients (see pages 115 and 119 in the text). Let's assume that you kept a record of the quantities needed when you made this recipe:

To get 1.25 kg EP onions, you needed 1.5 kg AP.
To get 600 g EP green pepper, you needed 700 g AP.

Chapter 12

Understanding Poultry and Game Birds

The subject of poultry is divided into two chapters, just as the subject of meats is. Unlike the first meat chapter, however, this first poultry chapter is quite short. One of the reasons for this is that there is not such a great variety of different cuts of poultry to learn as there is for meats. Furthermore, much of this chapter is taken up with trussing and cutting techniques, which need hands-on practice rather than written study questions.

After studying Chapter 12, you should be able to:

1. **Explain the differences between light meat and dark meat, and describe how these differences affect cooking.**
2. **Describe four techniques that help keep chicken or turkey breast moist while roasting.**
3. **Define the following terms used to classify poultry: *kind*, *class*, and *style*.**
4. **Identify popular types of farm-raised game birds and the cooking methods appropriate to their preparation.**
5. **Store poultry items.**
6. **Determine doneness in cooked poultry, both large roasted birds and smaller birds.**
7. **Truss poultry for cooking.**
8. **Cut chicken into parts.**

A. Terms

Fill in each blank with the term that is defined or described.

____________________ **1.** A government procedure that checks the wholesomeness of poultry, to make sure that it is fit to eat.

____________________ **2.** A government procedure that checks the quality of poultry.

_______________ 3. The market term indicating the amount of cleaning and processing a poultry item has had.

_______________ 4. The market term indicating the species (such as chicken, turkey, or duck) of a poultry item.

_______________ 5. The market term that indicates the relative age and sometimes the sex of a poultry item.

_______________ 6. A castrated male chicken.

_______________ 7. A mature female chicken.

_______________ 8. A mature male chicken.

_______________ 9. A young pigeon.

_______________ 10. A type of domestic poultry related to the pheasant.

_______________ 11. The process of tying the legs and wings of a poultry item against the body to make a compact shape for cooking.

_______________ 12. A common name for the nugget of tender meat in the hollow of the hip bone.

_______________ 13. A special breed of young chicken, often marketed at about 1 lb in weight.

_______________ 14. The boneless breast of a moulard duck.

B. Short-Answer Questions

1. A mature chicken of about 10 months of age is almost always cooked by what kind of cooking method? _______

2. Which of the major parts of a chicken has the most connective tissue? _______________

3. The highest Canadian grade of chicken is _______________ .

4. What is the best way to thaw a frozen capon that is vacuum packed in plastic? _______________

   ____

5. What is the weight range for young turkey? _______________

6. What class of duck is best for roasting, and what does one of these ducks weigh? _______________

7. At what temperature should frozen turkey be stored? ________

8. A large roasted bird is done when a meat thermometer inserted into ________________

registers the temperature of ________________.

9. Which disease-causing bacteria is most often associated with poultry? ________________ What precaution should be taken to avoid spreading this disease? ________________

____

10. What is the best way to hold fresh chickens in storage?

____

11. A chicken or other poultry item that is raised without various chemical growth enhancers or without certain antibiotics may be labeled ________________.

12. A chicken that is allowed to move around freely and eat outdoors in a more "natural" environment is called a ________________ chicken.

13. Two examples of ratites that appear on some menus are ________________ and ________________.

14. The game bird discussed in Chapter 12 that is closest to chicken in size and flavor is ________________.

15. If you were serving breast of wild duck on your menu, you would recommend to customers that it should be cooked to the ________________ stage of doneness because ________________

________________.

16. The protein in the muscles of poultry that makes "dark meat" dark is called ________________.

The purpose of this protein is to ________________,

therefore it is found in ________________ (more active or less active) muscles.

Chapter 13

Cooking Poultry and Game Birds

In this chapter, our examination shifts from product information to cooking techniques. The basic cooking methods, first discussed in Chapter 4, are applied to a range of poultry items.

After studying Chapter 13, you should be able to:

1. **Cook poultry by roasting and baking.**
2. **Cook poultry by broiling and grilling.**
3. **Cook poultry by sautéing, pan-frying, and deep-frying.**
4. **Cook poultry by simmering and poaching.**
5. **Cook poultry by braising.**
6. **Identify the safety, quality, and practicality concerns associated with preparing dressings and stuffings.**
7. **List basic ingredients for dressings and stuffings.**
8. **Prepare dressings and stuffings.**

A. Terms

Fill in each blank with the term that is defined or described.

______________________ 1. A chicken stew that is served with a pastry cover.

______________________ 2. A white chicken stew cooked by the braising method, but without browning the chicken, and served in a white sauce.

______________________ 3. A chicken stew prepared by the simmering method and served in a white sauce.

______________________ 4. A chicken stew as described in number 3, garnished with asparagus tips.

______________________ 5. A mature female chicken, which must be cooked by a moist-heat method to be made tender.

__________ 6. Chicken braised in red wine, garnished with small onions, mushrooms, and bacon.

__________ 7. Poultry that has been marinated, cooked in its own fat, then packed and stored in its own fat.

__________ 8. Grilled or sautéed poultry, meat, or seafood glazed with a soy sauce mixture.

__________ 9. Chicken served with a brown sauce flavored with white wine, shallots, mushrooms, and tomatoes.

__________ 10. The side of a piece of food that is to be face up on a plate when served.

__________ 11. A boneless chicken breast that has been pounded flat and then grilled.

__________ 12. A dish made of boneless chicken breast meat that has been chopped, mixed with heavy cream, molded into cutlet shapes, and pan-fried.

__________ 13. Classic French name for braised chicken with apples and cider.

__________ 14. A term for a stuffed boneless chicken leg.

__________ 15. Classic Spanish dish of chicken braised with rice.

__________ 16. Any of a variety of complex Mexican sauces that are cooked with chiles and other spices and that are usually thickened with corn or ground seeds or nuts.

__________ 17. To cook, covered, in an oven, basting regularly with butter, usually with a matignon for flavoring. Sometimes called *butter-roasting.*

B. Short-Answer Questions

1. What size chicken is best for deep-frying? __________

   ____

2. When you are sautéing a boneless breast of chicken, which side of the chicken breast should be browned first, for best appearance? __________

3. At what oven temperature should a 5-lb (2.3-kg) chicken be roasted? _____

4. A basic bread dressing or stuffing is made of __________, __________, __________, and __________, plus herbs, seasonings, and sometimes eggs.

5. If a chicken is stuffed before roasting, it is necessary to __________ the roasting time.

6. Baked, refrigerated poultry dressing that is to be heated for service must be reheated to an internal temperature of __________. The reason for this is __________

   __________.

7. ____________________ is a cooking method similar to simmering but requiring less liquid and a lower temperature.

8. To "flash-roast" a cornish game hen means to ____________________ .

9. A good temperature range for roasting large birds such as turkeys is ____________________ .

10. In a classic chicken fricassée, the sauce is enriched by adding a ____________________ , and it is seasoned with salt, white pepper, a little nutmeg, and lemon juice.

11. If grilled chicken becomes well browned on the outside before it is completely cooked on the inside, it may be finished by removing it from the grill and ____________________ ____________________ .

12. The deep-fryer should be set at a temperature of ____________ for deep-frying chicken.

13. Very small poultry items are generally roasted at a ____________________ temperature.

14. To "smoke-roast" a chicken breast means to ____________________ ____________________ .

15. Sautéed dishes made from game birds are most often made with the ____________ section of the bird only. They are usually cooked to the ____________________ stage of doneness.

C. Recipe Conversion

The following ingredients and quantities are for a Chicken à la King recipe that yields 25 portions at 8 oz each. Convert the recipe to the yields indicated.

	25 portions, 8 oz each	10 portions, 8 oz each	15 portions, 10 oz each
Butter, clarified	10 oz	________	________
Onion	3 oz	________	________
Green pepper	10 oz	________	________
Flour	8 oz	________	________
Chicken stock	2½ qt	________	________
Milk	2½ cups	________	________
Mushrooms	1 lb	________	________
Butter	4 oz	________	________
Light cream	2½ cups	________	________
Pimientos, drained	4 oz	________	________
Cooked chicken meat	5 lb	________	________
Sherry wine	4 oz	________	________
Salt	to taste	________	________
Pepper	to taste	________	________

Recipe Conversion—Metric

The following ingredients and quantities are for a Chicken à la King recipe that yields 25 portions at 250 g each. Convert the recipe to the yields indicated.

	25 portions, 250 g each	10 portions, 250 g each	15 portions, 300 g each
Butter, clarified	300 g	____________	____________
Onion	100 g	____________	____________
Green pepper	300 g	____________	____________
Flour	250 g	____________	____________
Chicken stock	2.5 L	____________	____________
Milk	650 mL	____________	____________
Mushrooms	500 g	____________	____________
Butter	125 g	____________	____________
Light cream	600 mL	____________	____________
Pimientos, drained	124 g	____________	____________
Cooked chicken meat	2.5 kg	____________	____________
Sherry wine	125 mL	____________	____________
Salt	to taste	____________	____________
Pepper	to taste	____________	____________

D. Portion Cost

In order to cost out the following recipe, we need to know the cost of cooked chicken meat. But let's assume we purchased and cooked fresh fowls in order to make the recipe. In order to cost the recipe, we first must do a cooked yield test, as discussed in Chapter 5 of the textbook, pages 118–119.

In the following shortened version of the cooked yield test form, use the figures given to calculate the cost per pound of the cooked chicken. Then use this figure to cost the recipe.

ITEM: **SIMMERED FRESH FOWL**

Net raw weight: 5 lb 4 oz   Cost per lb (raw): $ .89

Total net cost: $4.67

Weight as served (cooked meat): 1 lb 12 oz

Cooked cost per pound: ____________________

Cost out the following recipe. For prices of the ingredients, use figures supplied by your instructor or the *Sample Prices* in the Appendix of this *Study Guide*.

***ITEM:* CHICKEN TETRAZZINI**

Ingredient	Recipe Quantity	AP Quantity	Price	Total Amount
Cooked chicken	5 lb	________	________	________
Chicken stock	2½ qt	________	________	________
Flour	4 oz	________	________	________
Butter	10 oz	________	________	________
Mushrooms	2 lb	________	________	________
Egg yolks*	3	________	________	________
Heavy cream	2½ cups	________	________	________
Sherry	2 oz	________	________	________
Spaghetti	2½ lb	________	________	________
Parmesan cheese	8 oz	________	________	________
			Total cost	________
			Number of portions	40
			Cost per portion	________

**Note:* For the sake of this exercise, use the cost of whole eggs as the cost of the yolks. If you then use the egg whites in another recipe, you would enter a cost of zero for the whites when costing that recipe. This is because you are accounting for the cost of the whole eggs in the chicken recipe.

Portion Cost—Metric

In order to cost out the following recipe, we need to know the cost of cooked chicken meat. But let's assume we purchased and cooked fresh fowls in order to make the recipe. In order to cost the recipe, we first must do a cooked yield test, as discussed in Chapter 5 of the textbook, pages 118–119.

In the following shortened version of the cooked yield test form, use the figures given to calculate the cost per pound of the cooked chicken. Then use this figure to cost the recipe.

ITEM: **SIMMERED FRESH FOWL**

Net raw weight: 2.4 kg Cost per kg (raw): $1.95

Total net cost: $4.68

Weight as served (cooked meat): 800 g

Cooked cost per kilogram: ____________________

Cost out the following recipe. For prices of the ingredients, use figures supplied by your instructor or the *Sample Prices* in the Appendix of this *Study Guide*.

ITEM: **CHICKEN TETRAZZINI**

Ingredient	Recipe Quantity	AP Quantity	Price	Total Amount
Cooked chicken	2.5 kg	______	______	______
Chicken stock	2.5 L	______	______	______
Flour	125 g	______	______	______
Butter	300 g	______	______	______
Mushrooms	1 kg	______	______	______
Egg yolks*	3	______	______	______
Heavy cream	600 mL	______	______	______
Sherry	50 mL	______	______	______
Spaghetti	1.25 kg	______	______	______
Parmesan cheese	250 g	______	______	______
			Total cost	______
			Number of portions	40
			Cost per portion	______

**Note:* For the sake of this exercise, use the cost of whole eggs as the cost of the yolks. If you then use the egg whites in another recipe, you would enter a cost of zero for the whites when costing that recipe. This is because you are accounting for the cost of the whole eggs in the chicken recipe.

Chapter 14

Understanding Fish and Shellfish

The composition and structure of fish and seafood products is quite different from that of meat and poultry. Furthermore, fish products are much more perishable than meat is. Consequently, this subject requires special study, so that when you apply the basic cooking techniques to seafood products, you will be able to adjust them to fit these unique products.

After studying Chapter 14, you should be able to:

1. **Explain how the cooking qualities of fish are affected by the lack of connective tissue.**
2. **Determine doneness in cooked fish.**
3. **Demonstrate the appropriate cooking methods for fat and lean fish.**
4. **List the seven basic market forms of fish.**
5. **Dress and fillet round fish and flat fish.**
6. **List and describe common varieties of saltwater and freshwater fin fish used in North American food service.**
7. **Identify the characteristics of fresh fish, and contrast them with characteristics of not-so-fresh fish.**
8. **Store fish and fish products.**
9. **Identify the popular varieties of shellfish and discuss their characteristics.**
10. **Outline the special safe handling and cooking procedures for shellfish.**
11. **Open clams and oysters, split lobster, and peel and devein shrimp.**

A. Terms

Fill in each blank with the term that is defined or described.

_______________ 1. The family of sea animals that includes soft animals that live inside a pair of hinged shells.

_______________ 2. The family of sea animals that have segmented shells and jointed legs.

_______________ **3.** The smallest size of Eastern hard-shell clams.

_______________ **4.** The largest size of Eastern hard-shell clams.

_______________ **5.** In bivalves (animals with a pair of hinged shells), the muscle that closes the shells.

_______________ **6.** The pale green liver of a lobster.

_______________ **7.** The largest of the crabs.

_______________ **8.** The roe or eggs of a lobster.

_______________ **9.** The inactive, dying lobster.

_______________ **10.** The words that the abbreviation IQF stands for.

____

____

_______________ **11.** Market term for raw shrimp in the shell.

_______________ **12.** A blue crab that was harvested just after it molted or shed its shell.

_______________ **13.** The words that the abbreviation PDC, as applied to shrimp, stands for.

____

____

_______________ **14.** Coated with a thin layer of ice when frozen, in order to prevent drying.

_______________ **15.** A fresh-water shellfish that looks like a small lobster.

_______________ **16.** A small relative of the rock lobster, sometimes sold as rock shrimp.

_______________ **17.** The Italian name for squid, often used on menus.

_______________ **18.** The name for the family of mollusks that includes squid, cuttlefish, and octopus.

_______________ **19.** The general name for a processed seafood product that is made by grinding lean, white fish and shaping it to resemble crab legs and other shellfish.

_______________ **20.** Designating fish that live in salt water but that swim into fresh water to lay eggs.

_______________ **21.** Designating fish that live in fresh water but that swim into salt water to lay eggs.

B. Fin Fish: Market Forms

In the blanks, write the name of the market form that corresponds to the description and illustration.

1. ______________________ Viscera removed

2. ______________________ Boneless side of fish

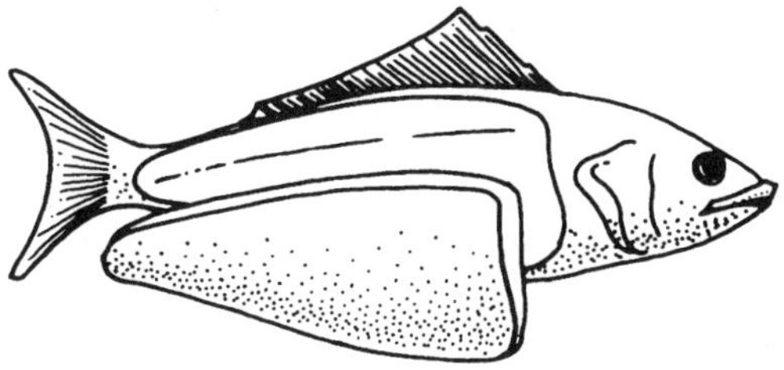

3. ______________________ Completely intact, as caught

4. ______________________ Cross-section slices

5. ______________________ Viscera, scales, head, tail, and fins removed

6. ______________________ Both sides of fish joined, bones removed

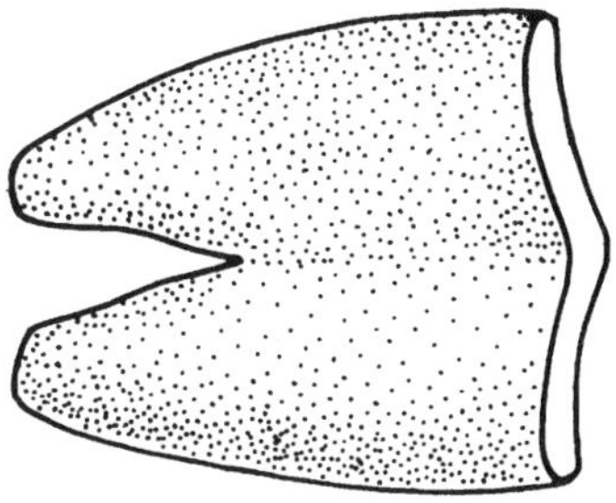

C. Fat Fish and Lean Fish

In the blank before the name of each fish, write the word "lean" if the fish is low in fat; write the word "fat" if it is high in fat.

1. ____________________ Haddock
2. ____________________ Salmon
3. ____________________ Ocean perch
4. ____________________ Red snapper
5. ____________________ Tuna
6. ____________________ Swordfish
7. ____________________ Pompano
8. ____________________ Pike
9. ____________________ Shad
10. ____________________ Black sea bass
11. ____________________ Chilean sea bass
12. ____________________ Whiting
13. ____________________ Whitefish
14. ____________________ Flounder
15. ____________________ Sole
16. ____________________ Cod
17. ____________________ Escolar
18. ____________________ Trout
19. ____________________ Halibut
20. ____________________ Bluefish
21. ____________________ Mackerel
22. ____________________ Tilefish
23. ____________________ Monkfish
24. ____________________ Eel
25. ____________________ Skate
26. ____________________ John Dory
27. ____________________ Mahi-mahi
28. ____________________ Red mullet
29. ____________________ Tilapia

D. Review: Freshness and Storage

1. List five signs of freshness in whole fin fish.

   (a) ______

   (b) ______

   (c) ______

   (d) ______

   (e) ______

2. What is the most important sign of freshness in fish fillets?

   ______

3. What is the most important sign of freshness in lobsters?

   ______

4. What is the most important sign of freshness in clams, oysters, and mussels? ______

   ______

5. What is the best way to store whole fin fish?

   ______

6. At what temperature should frozen fish be stored?

   ______

7. What is the best way to thaw frozen fish? ______

   ______

8. What is the best way to store fresh clams and oysters in the shell? ______

   ______

9. What are two ways of storing live lobsters?

(a) ______________________________

(b) ______________________________

10. What is the best way to store thawed raw shrimp in the shell?

____

E. True/False

T F **1.** Haddock is an example of flatfish.

T F **2.** In general, fat fish are better suited for broiling than lean fish are.

T F **3.** In fish cookery, moist-heat methods are used primarily to tenderize tough fish.

T F **4.** Some canned fish products are inspected for wholesomeness by the federal government.

T F **5.** Shrimp that are designated "21/25" weigh about 1¼ oz each.

T F **6.** A fish that is very fresh has clear, white gills.

T F **7.** The largest varieties of scallops are called sea scallops.

T F **8.** Frozen fish fillets must be completely thawed before they can be breaded.

T F **9.** Scallops are available only in the fall, winter, and spring.

T F **10.** If baked clams are tough, it is because they weren't cooked long enough.

Chapter 15

Cooking Fish and Shellfish

This chapter applies the basic cooking techniques to seafood products. Keeping in mind that the structure of fish is quite different from that of meat and poultry, pay special attention to the ways in which cooking fish differs from cooking meats.

After studying Chapter 15, you should be able to:

1. **Cook fish and shellfish by baking.**
2. **Cook fish and shellfish by broiling.**
3. **Cook fish and shellfish by sautéing and pan-frying.**
4. **Cook fish and shellfish by deep-frying.**
5. **Cook fish and shellfish by poaching in court bouillon.**
6. **Cook fish and shellfish by poaching in fumet and wine.**
7. **Cook fish and shellfish by mixed cooking techniques.**
8. **Prepare dishes made of raw seafood.**

A. Terms

Fill in each blank with the term that is defined or described.

____________________ **1.** Water containing seasonings, herbs, and usually an acid, used for cooking fish.

____________________ **2.** Trout that was alive until cooking time and that turns blue when cooked in water containing an acid such as lemon juice or vinegar.

____________________ **3.** A dish consisting of chopped raw fish mixed with seasoning.

____________________ **4.** Fish dredged in flour, sautéed in butter, and served with a topping of lemon juice, parsley, and browned butter.

____________________ **5.** A dish consisting of poached fish on a bed of spinach, topped with Mornay sauce.

_________________ **6.** A term referring to fish topped with a rich sauce and browned under a broiler or salamander.

_________________ **7.** Mussels steamed with white wine, shallots, and parsley.

_________________ **8.** A dish consisting of fish or seafood served in a cream sauce flavored with sherry or other fortified wine.

_________________ **9.** A French term meaning "to cook a product in its own juices; to sweat."

_________________ **10.** Wrapped in paper for cooking so that the food is steamed in its own moisture.

_________________ **11.** Thin, flat items such as fish fillets rolled up into tight rolls, then cooked and served in this fashion.

_________________ **12.** French menu name for poached sole in white wine sauce.

_________________ **13.** Dish similar to the one described in number 11, but with the addition of mushrooms.

_________________ **14.** A dish consisting of trout prepared as described in number 3 but garnished with browned sliced almonds.

_________________ **15.** A dish consisting of cut-up lobster sautéed and then cooked and served in a sauce made with tomato, shallot, garlic, white wine, brandy, fish stock, and herbs.

_________________ **16.** A style of preparation in which a poached fish or seafood item is served "swimming" in a broth made of its poaching liquid.

_________________ **17.** A dish consisting of thin slices of raw fish pounded paper-thin, served with a piquant cold sauce.

_________________ **18.** French term for a cooking liquid.

_________________ **19.** A Japanese deep-fried dish characterized by a very light batter.

B. Review of Shallow Poaching Fish in Wine

The following are the steps in the procedure for poaching fish in wine and fish stock, but they are out of order. Place them in the correct order by writing the number "1" in front of the first step, "2" in front of the second step, and so on.

_______ Butter the bottom of the pan.

_______ Reduce the poaching liquid to about one-fourth of its volume.

_______ Strain the sauce.

_______ Sprinkle chopped shallots into the pan.

_______ Add enough fish fumet and white wine to almost cover the fish.

_______ Monter au beurre. Season with salt, white pepper, and lemon juice.

_______ Collect all equipment and food supplies.

_______ Plate the fish and coat with the sauce.

_______ Cover the fish and bring the liquid to a simmer.

_______ Arrange the fish portions in the pan in a single layer. Season them lightly.

_______ Poach the fish, covered, in the oven or on the range at moderate heat.

_______ Add fish velouté and heavy cream. Bring to a simmer and season with salt, white pepper, and lemon juice.

_______ Drain the poaching liquid into another pan. Keep the fish warm.

_______ Add a tempered liaison.

C. Short-Answer Questions

1. When you are sautéing a fillet of fish, which side of the fillet should be browned first? _______________

   ____.

2. The breading on deep-fried fish serves several purposes. List three purposes.

   (a) ____

   (b) ____

   (c) ____

3. Besides mirepoix and various seasonings, herbs, and spices, the two main ingredients in a court bouillon for cooking fish are _______________ and _______________.

4. Plain fish steaks to be baked or broiled are usually coated with _______________ before cooking.

5. What is the normal oven temperature range for baking fish? _______________

6. The main flavoring ingredient for scampi-style broiled shrimp is _______________.

7. Whole fish to be served cold on a buffet are usually cooked by what method? _______________

8. When you are rolling up sole fillets to prepare them for cooking, which side of the fillet should be on the inside of the roll? _______________

9. The preferred fats for sautéing fish are oil and _______________.

10. Fish to be sautéed à la meunière is often soaked in _______________ before dredging it in _______________. This helps form a crust that browns nicely.

11. List five guidelines for food safety when preparing and serving dishes made of raw seafood.

(a) ____________________

(b) ____________________

(c) ____________________

(d) ____________________

(e) ____________________

12. The main ingredient in sushi is ____________________ .

13. ____________________ is a dish made by marinating raw seafood in ____________________ until it has the texture of cooked fish.

D. Recipe Conversion

The following ingredients and quantities are for a Baked Clam recipe that yields 10 portions at 3 clams each. Convert the recipe to the yields indicated.

	10 portions, 3 clams each	30 portions, 3 clams each	30 portions, 4 clams each
Cherrystone clams	30	__________	__________
Olive oil	2 oz	__________	__________
Shallots	1½ oz	__________	__________
Garlic, chopped	1 tsp	__________	__________
Lemon juice	5 tsp	__________	__________
Bread crumbs, fresh	10 oz	__________	__________
Chopped parsley	1 tbsp	__________	__________
Oregano	¾ tsp	__________	__________
White pepper	⅛ tsp	__________	__________
Parmesan cheese	⅓ cup	__________	__________
Lemon wedges	10	__________	__________

Recipe Conversion—Metric

The following ingredients and quantities are for a Baked Clam recipe that yields 10 portions at 3 clams each. Convert the recipe to the yields indicated.

	10 portions, 3 clams each	**30 portions, 3 clams each**	**30 portions, 4 clams each**
Cherrystone clams	30	____________	____________
Olive oil	60 mL	____________	____________
Shallots	50 g	____________	____________
Garlic, chopped	5 mL	____________	____________
Lemon juice	25 mL	____________	____________
Bread crumbs, fresh	300 g	____________	____________
Chopped parsley	15 mL	____________	____________
Oregano	3 mL	____________	____________
White pepper	0.5 mL	____________	____________
Parmesan cheese	75 mL	____________	____________
Lemon wedges	10	____________	____________

E. Portion Cost

Cost out the following recipe. For prices of the ingredients, use figures supplied by your instructor or the *Sample Prices* in the Appendix of this *Study Guide*.

ITEM: **POACHED SOLE FILLETS BONNE FEMME**

Ingredient	Recipe Quantity	AP Quantity	Price	Total Amount
Sole fillets	6¼ lb	______	______	______
Butter	7 oz	______	______	______
Flour	4 oz	______	______	______
Fish stock	3 cups	______	______	______
Shallots*	3 oz	______	______	______
Mushrooms*	1½ lb	______	______	______
Heavy cream	12 oz	______	______	______
			Total cost	______
			Number of portions	25
			Cost per portion	______

**Note:* Remember that you need AP weights of all ingredients (see pages 115 and 119 in the text). Let's assume that you kept a record of the quantities needed when you made this recipe:

To get 3 oz EP shallots, you needed 4 oz AP.

To get 1½ lb EP mushrooms, you needed 1 lb 10 oz AP.

Portion Cost—Metric

Cost out the following recipe. For prices of the ingredients, use figures supplied by your instructor or the *Sample Prices* in the Appendix of this *Study Guide*.

ITEM: **POACHED SOLE FILLETS BONNE FEMME**

Ingredient	Recipe Quantity	AP Quantity	Price	Total Amount
Sole fillets	3 kg	________	________	________
Butter	200 g	________	________	________
Flour	125 g	________	________	________
Fish stock	750 mL	________	________	________
Shallots*	100 g	________	________	________
Mushrooms*	700 g	________	________	________
Heavy cream	350 mL	________	________	________
			Total cost	________
			Number of portions	25
			Cost per portion	________

**Note:* Remember that you need AP weights of all ingredients (see pages 115 and 119 in the text). Let's assume that you kept a record of the quantities needed when you made this recipe:

To get 100 g EP shallots, you needed 125 g AP.

To get 700 g EP mushrooms, you needed 750 g AP.

Chapter 16

Understanding Vegetables

The material on vegetables and starches is divided into four chapters. While each of these four chapters of exercises is relatively short, together they contain many important points to study and review.

After studying Chapter 16, you should be able to:

1. **Describe the factors that influence texture, flavor, color, and nutritional changes when cooking vegetables.**
2. **Cook vegetables to their proper doneness.**
3. **Judge quality in cooked vegetables based on color, appearance, texture, flavor, seasonings, and appropriateness of combination with sauces or other vegetables.**
4. **Perform pre-preparation tasks for fresh vegetables.**
5. **Determine the quality of frozen, canned, and dried vegetables.**
6. **Prepare vegetables using the batch cooking method and the blanch-and-chill method.**
7. **Store both fresh and processed vegetables.**

A. Terms

Fill in each blank with the term that is defined or described.

______________________ 1. Compounds that give vegetables their color.

______________________ 2. Firm to the bite, not soft or mushy; a term used to describe the texture of vegetables and some other foods that are cooked to this stage of doneness.

______________________ 3. The compound that colors green vegetables green.

______________________ 4. The weight of the solids, minus the juice, in a can of vegetables or fruits.

_________________ **5.** The size of the individual pieces in a can of vegetables (for example, the diameter of the peas in a can).

_________________ **6.** The compounds that color carrots and sweet potatoes orange.

_________________ **7.** The compounds that color tomatoes and red peppers red.

_________________ **8.** The compounds that color corn yellow.

_________________ **9.** The compounds that color beets and red cabbage red.

_________________ **10.** The compounds that color cauliflower and potatoes white.

_________________ **11.** The fuzzy center of an artichoke.

_________________ **12.** Dried, discolored spots on frozen foods due to improper storage or packaging.

_________________ **13.** A kitchen procedure that involves dividing a large quantity of a food item into several smaller containers and cooking each one separately as needed.

_________________ **14.** A kitchen procedure that involves partially cooking foods ahead of time, refrigerating them, then finishing portions of the foods as needed at service time.

_________________ **15.** A mature cremini mushroom with a cap that forms a broad, thick, flat disk that may be as large as 6 inches (15 cm) or more across.

_________________ **16.** A popular wild mushroom that is cone-shaped and hollow.

_________________ **17.** The fresh version of the dried Chinese black mushroom.

_________________ **18.** A golden-yellow wild mushroom shaped like an inside-out umbrella and with ridges instead of gills.

B. Short-Answer Questions

1. If green beans are cooked with lemon juice, their color will turn _________________ .

2. When peas are harvested, their _________________ content begins to change to starch.

3. Frozen vegetables should be stored at a temperature of _________________ .

4. Baking soda added to cooking water makes the texture of vegetables _________________ .

5. Cut surfaces of artichokes are rubbed with _________________ so that they will not turn brown.

6. Rutabagas should be cooked uncovered so that _________________________________

   _________________________________ .

7. The top of a can of vegetables should be _________________ before it is opened.

8. A bulging can of green beans should be _________________________________ .

9. Vitamins in vegetables can be lost or destroyed by

(a) ______________________, (b) ______________________,

(c) ______________________, (d) ______________________,

(e) ______________________, and (f) ______________________.

10. Vegetables should be cut into neat, uniform shapes for better appearance and for ______________.

11. When fresh peas are added to cooking water, the temperature of the water should be ______________.

12. The bottom portions of asparagus stalks are ______________ so that the asparagus will cook more evenly.

13. Frozen vegetables need less cooking time than fresh vegetables because ______________.

14. Two or more batches of cooked vegetables should not be mixed together because ______________

____.

15. Five examples of hot peppers or chiles are __________, __________, __________, __________,

and __________.

16. Before dried mushrooms are used in a recipe, they should be ______________

____.

17. The most important reason never to use a wild mushroom that hasn't been definitely identified by an expert is

____.

C. Math Exercise: Trimming Loss

The exercises below are of two kinds, calculating yield and calculating amount needed. To do the calculations, you need to know the percentage yield for each vegetable, as listed in Chapter 16 of the text. For your convenience, the necessary percentages are repeated here.

These calculations are explained in Chapter 5 of the text, in the section titled "Trimming Loss: Calculating Yields and Amounts Needed." Review this section if necessary.

Artichokes, Jerusalem	80%
Asparagus	55%
Beans, green	88%
Broccoli	70%
Cabbage	80%
Celery	75%

Eggplant	75% (peeled)
Kohlrabi	55%
Leeks	50%
Mushrooms	90%
Okra	82%
Onions, dry	90%
Peas	40%
Potatoes	80%
Turnips	75%
Zucchini	90%

Calculating Amount Needed

Assume you need the following quantities, EP, of the indicated fresh vegetables. Calculate the AP weight you will need to get the required yield. (Questions 1–10 use U.S. measures; questions 11–20 use metric measures. Answer whichever questions are assigned by your instructor.)

	EP Weight Desired	AP Weight Needed
1. Kohlrabi	1 lb	__________
2. Potatoes	12 oz	__________
3. Jerusalem artichokes	1 lb	__________
4. Eggplant, peeled	2½ lb	__________
5. Leeks	6 oz	__________
6. Okra	8 oz	__________
7. Onions, dry	1½ lb	__________
8. Mushrooms	1 lb	__________
9. Celery	3 lb	__________
10. Zucchini	2 lb	__________

	EP Weight Desired	AP Weight Needed
11. Kohlrabi	500 g	________
12. Potatoes	400 g	________
13. Jerusalem artichokes	450 g	________
14. Eggplant, peeled	1.25 kg	________
15. Leeks	200 g	________
16. Okra	250 g	________
17. Onions, dry	700 g	________
18. Mushrooms	475 g	________
19. Celery	1.5 kg	________
20. Zucchini	900 g	________

Calculating Yield

Assume you have the following quantities, AP, of the indicated fresh vegetables. Calculate the EP weight you will have left after trimming. (Questions 21–30 use U.S. measures; questions 31–40 use metric measures. Answer whichever questions are assigned by your instructor.)

	AP Weight	EP Weight
21. Asparagus	12 oz	________
22. Red cabbage	6 lb	________
23. Mushrooms	2½ lb	________
24. Green beans	1½ lb	________
25. Peas	4½ lb	________
26. Turnips	2 lb	________
27. Broccoli	2½ lb	________
28. Leeks	6 lb	________
29. Okra	1 lb	________
30. Zucchini	5 lb	________
31. Asparagus	375 g	________
32. Red cabbage	3 kg	________
33. Mushrooms	1.25 kg	________

34. Green beans	700 g	________
35. Peas	2.2 kg	________
36. Turnips	450 g	________
37. Broccoli	1.2 kg	________
38. Leeks	2.75 kg	________
39. Okra	500 g	________
40. Zucchini	2.75 kg	________

Chapter 17

Cooking Vegetables

This chapter continues your review of vegetables, concentrating on cooking techniques. After studying Chapter 17, you should be able to:

1. **Identify vegetables that are well suited to the different vegetable cooking methods.**
2. **Cook vegetables by boiling and steaming.**
3. **Cook vegetables by sautéing and pan-frying.**
4. **Cook vegetables by braising.**
5. **Cook vegetables by baking.**
6. **Cook vegetables by broiling and grilling.**
7. **Cook vegetables by deep-frying.**

A. Terms

Fill in each blank with the term that is defined or described.

______________________ 1. A style of vegetable preparation in which the vegetables are topped with browned sliced almonds.

______________________ 2. A style of vegetable preparation in which the vegetable preparation is covered with a topping, such as a sauce, cheese, and/or bread crumbs, and browned under a boiler or salamander.

______________________ 3. A dish consisting of braised sauerkraut served with a variety of sausages and other pork products.

______________________ 4. A general term referring to foods coated with or mixed with a batter and deep-fried.

______________________ 5. To give a vegetable a shiny coating by cooking it with sugar and butter or with a syrup.

________________ 6. Thick vegetable purées or mixtures of small pieces of vegetable and a heavy béchamel or other binder, formed into shapes, breaded, and fried.

________________ 7. A style of vegetable preparation in which the vegetable is topped with chopped hard-cooked egg, chopped parsley, and bread crumbs browned in butter.

________________ 8. A vegetable stew made of eggplant, tomatoes, onions, peppers, and zucchini.

________________ 9. Artichoke bottoms filled with peas.

________________ 10. A coarse paste or hash made of finely chopped mushrooms sautéed with shallots.

________________ 11. Peas cooked with pearl onions and shredded lettuce in a lightly bound white stock.

________________ 12. A method of cooking vegetables in a small amount of water in a covered pan so that they partly steam and partly boil.

B. True/False

T F 1. One advantage of cooking vegetables in a pressure steamer is that the door can be opened at any time to check on the vegetables.

T F 2. Simmering is better than boiling for vegetables that can be easily broken.

T F 3. If green peas are not to be served soon after they are boiled, they should be cooled in cold water and refrigerated until needed.

T F 4. Zucchini must be parboiled before being sautéed.

T F 5. Sautéing is similar to pan-frying, except that sautéing always requires more fat.

T F 6. To sauté vegetables, set the sauté pan over moderate heat, add the butter and vegetables, then wait until the pan gets hot before flipping the vegetables.

T F 7. Braised vegetables are browned in fat, then cooked slowly in a small amount of liquid.

T F 8. The difference between braised meat and braised vegetables is that mirepoix is never used with vegetables.

T F 9. Vinegar is added to braised red cabbage to flavor it and to enhance its red color.

T F 10. Quick-cooking vegetables are best for broiling.

T F 11. All vegetables that are coated in batter and deep-fried must first be blanched or parboiled.

T F 12. Deep-fried vegetables are best if cooked to order.

T F 13. Perforated pans should never be used for steaming vegetables, because too many juices will be lost.

T F 14. Creamed spinach is made by cooking fresh spinach in a cream sauce.

C. Recipe Conversion

The following ingredients and quantities are for a Braised Red Cabbage recipe that yields 25 portions at 5 oz each. Convert the recipe to the yields indicated.

	25 portions, 5 oz each	**10 portions, 5 oz each**	**15 portions, 4 oz each**
Red cabbage, AP	6 lb	______	______
Bacon	12 oz	______	______
Onions	1 lb	______	______
Sugar	1 oz	______	______
White stock	1½ pt	______	______
Apples, cored and diced	1 lb	______	______
Cloves	4	______	______
Whole allspice	6	______	______
Stick cinnamon	1 piece	______	______
Red wine vinegar	4 oz	______	______
Red wine	1 cup	______	______
Salt	to taste	______	______
Pepper	to taste	______	______

Recipe Conversion—Metric

The following ingredients and quantities are for a Braised Red Cabbage recipe that yields 25 portions at 125 g each. Convert the recipe to the yields indicated.

	25 portions, 125 g each	**10 portions, 125 g each**	**15 portions, 100 g each**
Red cabbage, AP	2.5 kg	______	______
Bacon	350 g	______	______
Onions	400 g	______	______
Sugar	25 g	______	______
White stock	700 mL	______	______
Apples, cored and diced	400 g	______	______
Cloves	4	______	______
Whole allspice	6	______	______
Stick cinnamon	1 piece	______	______
Red wine vinegar	100 mL	______	______
Red wine	250 mL	______	______
Salt	to taste	______	______
Pepper	to taste	______	______

D. Portion Cost

Cost out the following recipes. For prices of the ingredients, use figures supplied by your instructor or the *Sample Prices* in the Appendix of this *Study Guide*.

***ITEM:* ARTICHOKES CLAMART**

Ingredient	Recipe Quantity	AP Quantity	Price	Total Amount
Artichokes	10	________	________	________
Lemons	2	________	________	________
Flour	1 oz	________	________	________
Cold water	3 pt	________	________	________
Salt	½ oz	________	________	________
Peas, frozen	10 oz	________	________	________
Butter	3 oz	________	________	________
			Total cost	________
			Number of portions	10
			Cost per portion	________

***ITEM:* GLAZED CARROTS**

Ingredient	Recipe Quantity	AP Quantity	Price	Total Amount
Carrots, AP	6½ lb	________	________	________
Butter	3 oz	________	________	________
Sugar	2 oz	________	________	________
			Total cost	________
			Number of portions	25
			Cost per portion	________

***ITEM:* PUREED BUTTERNUT SQUASH**

Ingredient	Recipe Quantity	AP Quantity	Price	Total Amount
Butternut squash	10 lb	________	________	________
Butter	8 oz	________	________	________
Brown sugar	4 oz	________	________	________
Salt	½ oz	________	________	________
			Total cost	________
			Number of portions	25
			Cost per portion	________

Portion Cost—Metric

Cost out the following recipes. For prices of the ingredients, use figures supplied by your instructor or the *Sample Prices* in the Appendix of this *Study Guide*.

***ITEM:* ARTICHOKES CLAMART**

Ingredient	Recipe Quantity	AP Quantity	Price	Total Amount
Artichokes	10	________	________	________
Lemons	2	________	________	________
Flour	30 g	________	________	________
Cold water	1.5 l	________	________	________
Salt	15 g	________	________	________
Peas, frozen	300 g	________	________	________
Butter	90 g	________	________	________
			Total cost	________
			Number of portions	10
			Cost per portion	________

ITEM: **GLAZED CARROTS**

Ingredient	Recipe Quantity	AP Quantity	Price	Total Amount
Carrots, AP	3 kg	________	________	________
Butter	100 g	________	________	________
Sugar	60 g	________	________	________
			Total cost	________
			Number of portions	25
			Cost per portion	________

ITEM: **PUREED BUTTERNUT SQUASH**

Ingredient	Recipe Quantity	AP Quantity	Price	Total Amount
Butternut squash	5 kg	________	________	________
Butter	250 g	________	________	________
Brown sugar	125 g	________	________	________
Salt	15 g	________	________	________
			Total cost	________
			Number of portions	25
			Cost per portion	________

Chapter 18

Potatoes

The last of three chapters covering basic vegetable cookery, this unit concentrates on potatoes. The importance of potatoes in our diet suggests that a thorough review of this material is important.

After studying Chapter 18, you should be able to:

1. **Classify potatoes into two types, describe the general properties of each type, and identify the most suitable cooking method for each type.**
2. **Identify characteristics of high-quality potatoes, and describe how to store them.**
3. **Cook potatoes by boiling and steaming.**
4. **Prepare potato purée.**
5. **Cook potatoes by baking, sautéing, pan-frying, and deep-frying.**

A. Terms

Fill in each blank with the term that is defined or described.

____________________ 1. A variety of potato, often from Idaho, having a high starch content and often used for baking.

____________________ 2. General term for potatoes that are low in starch and high in sugar, with a firm, moist texture.

____________________ 3. A poisonous substance present in the green parts found in some potatoes.

____________________ 4. Another name for immature potatoes.

____________________ 5. Long, narrow, finger-shaped potato.

____________________ 6. Name given to many classical dishes featuring the potato, after the French pharmacist who promoted the use of the potato in the eighteenth century.

____________________ 7. Potato purée mixed with egg yolk and butter, piped with a pastry bag and browned under a salamander.

B. Classic Potato Preparations

Column 1 below is a list of descriptions of various classic potato dishes. Column 2 is a list of the names of these dishes. Match the names to the descriptions by writing the letter of the correct name in the space before the description.

_______ 1. Potato purée combined with butter and egg yolks, often used for decorative work

_______ 2. Sliced potatoes baked with cream, milk, and cheese

_______ 3. Cooked potatoes chopped, formed into cakes, and pan-fried

_______ 4. Trimmed potatoes simmered in stock with onion and carrot

_______ 5. Mixture of duchesse potatoes and pâte à choux, deep-fried

_______ 6. Small tournéed potatoes browned in butter

_______ 7. Thin, matchstick-sized french fries

_______ 8. Plain boiled potatoes

_______ 9. Same as number 5 but flavored with parmesan cheese

_______ 10. Cut with ball cutter and browned in butter

_______ 11. Sliced potatoes arranged in overlapping rings in a pan and baked with butter

_______ 12. Sliced potatoes and onions moistened with stock and baked with roast lamb

_______ 13. Baked in cheese sauce until browned on top

_______ 14. Duchesse mixture shaped, breaded, and deep-fried

_______ 15. Sliced, boiled potatoes pan-fried with onions

_______ 16. Diced potatoes pan-fried with bacon, onion, green pepper, and pimiento

_______ 17. Steamed potatoes

_______ 18. Baked potatoes puréed with butter, made into cakes, and pan-fried

_______ 19. Boiled potatoes sliced and pan-fried

_______ 20. Potatoes sliced on a mandoline into waffle shapes, deep-fried until crisp

a. Rissolé or Cocotte
b. Dauphine Potatoes
c. Parisienne or Noisette
d. Duchesse Potatoes
e. au Gratin
f. Boulangère
g. Home Fries
h. O'Brien
i. Croquettes
j. Lyonnaise
k. Hashed Browns
l. Allumette
m. Dauphinoise
n. Anna
o. Bouillon
p. Gaufrette
q. Macaire
r. Pommes Vapeurs
s. Lorette
t. Pommes Natures

C. Short-Answer Questions

1. List six characteristics of a high-quality potato.

   (a) ______________________________

   (b) ______________________________

   (c) ______________________________

   (d) ______________________________

   (e) ______________________________

   (f) ______________________________

2. At what temperature should potatoes be stored? ________

3. The following are steps in the procedure for making potato purée for duchesse potatoes. Fill in the missing step.

   (a) Wash, peel, and eye. Cut into uniform sizes.

   (b) Simmer until tender.

   (c) Drain in colander.

   (d) ______________________________

   (e) Pass through a food mill to purée.

4. How are french fries blanched? ______________________________

   ____

   ____

5. Why should starchy potatoes not be refrigerated? ______________________________

   ____

6. What is the easiest and most commonly used method for preventing potatoes from turning brown after they have been peeled or cut? ______________________________

   ____

7. What kind of potatoes are most often used for making potato purée—starchy or waxy? ______________

   Why? ______________________________

   ____

8. What are the four principal colors of potatoes?

____

____

____

____

9. What is likely to happen to potato purée if it is mixed too much? _______________

____

D. Recipe Conversion

The following ingredients and quantities are for Hungarian Potatoes, yielding 25 portions, 4 oz each. Convert the recipe to the yields indicated.

	25 portions, 4 oz each	15 portions, 4 oz each	15 portions, 5 oz each
Butter	4 oz	______	______
Onion	8 oz	______	______
Paprika	2 tsp	______	______
Tomato concassée	1 lb	______	______
Potatoes, peeled	5 lb	______	______
Chicken stock	1 qt	______	______
Salt	to taste	______	______
Pepper	to taste	______	______
Chopped parsley	½ cup	______	______

The following ingredients and quantities are for a recipe for Potatoes au Gratin, yielding 25 portions at 6 oz each. Convert the recipe to the yields indicated.

	25 portions, 6 oz each	15 portions, 6 oz each	25 portions, 4 oz each
Potatoes, all-purpose	7½ lb	______	______
Cheese sauce	2 qt	______	______
Dry bread crumbs	⅔ cup	______	______
Paprika	2 tsp	______	______
Butter, melted	2 oz	______	______

Recipe Conversion—Metric

The following ingredients and quantities are for a recipe for Hungarian Potatoes, yielding 25 portions at 100 g each. Convert the recipe to the yields indicated.

	25 portions, 100 g each	15 portions, 100 g each	15 portions, 125 g each
Butter	100 g	________	________
Onion	200 g	________	________
Paprika	10 mL	________	________
Tomato concassée	400 g	________	________
Potatoes, peeled	2 kg	________	________
Chicken stock	800 mL	________	________
Salt	to taste	________	________
Pepper	to taste	________	________
Chopped parsley	100 mL	________	________

The following ingredients and quantities are for a recipe for Potatoes au Gratin, yielding 25 portions at 175 g each. Convert the recipe to the yields indicated.

	25 portions, 175 g each	15 portions, 175 g each	25 portions, 125 g each
Potatoes, all-purpose	3.5 kg	________	________
Cheese sauce	2 L	________	________
Dry bread crumbs	150 mL	________	________
Paprika	10 mL	________	________
Butter, melted	60 g	________	________

E. Portion Cost

Cost out the following recipes. For prices of the ingredients, use figures supplied by your instructor or the *Sample Prices* in the Appendix of this *Study Guide*.

ITEM: **BOULANGERE POTATOES**

Ingredient	Recipe Quantity	AP Quantity	Price	Total Amount
Onions, AP	2½ lb	________	________	________
Butter	5 oz	________	________	________
Potatoes, all-purpose, AP	7½ lb	________	________	________
Chicken stock	1 qt	________	________	________
			Total cost	________
			Number of portions	25
			Cost per portion	________

ITEM: **POTATO PANCAKES**

Ingredient	Recipe Quantity	AP Quantity	Price	Total Amount
Potatoes, all-purpose	6 lb	________	________	________
Onions	1 lb	________	________	________
Lemons	2	________	________	________
Eggs	6	________	________	________
Flour, all-purpose	2 oz	________	________	________
			Total cost	________
			Number of portions	20
			Cost per portion	________

Portion Cost—Metric

Cost out the following recipes. For prices of the ingredients, use figures supplied by your instructor or the *Sample Prices* in the Appendix of this *Study Guide*.

ITEM: BOULANGERE POTATOES

Ingredient	Recipe Quantity	AP Quantity	Price	Total Amount
Onions, AP	1.2 kg	______	______	______
Butter	150 g	______	______	______
Potatoes, all-purpose, AP	3.6 kg	______	______	______
Chicken stock	1 L	______	______	______
			Total cost	______
			Number of portions	25
			Cost per portion	______

ITEM: POTATO PANCAKES

Ingredient	Recipe Quantity	AP Quantity	Price	Total Amount
Potatoes, all-purpose	2.7 kg	______	______	______
Onions	450 g	______	______	______
Lemons	2	______	______	______
Eggs	6	______	______	______
Flour, all-purpose	60 g	______	______	______
			Total cost	______
			Number of portions	20
			Cost per portion	______

Chapter 19

Legumes, Grains, Pasta, and Other Starches

This chapter continues the study of starch products that was begun with the discussion of potatoes in Chapter 18. The three main sections in this chapter are dried legumes, grains, and pasta or noodle products. In addition, various dumplings are introduced.

After studying Chapter 19, you should be able to:

1. **Distinguish the major types of dried legumes.**
2. **Cook dried legumes.**
3. **Distinguish the major types of rice.**
4. **Distinguish the major types of other grains used in food service.**
5. **Prepare grains by simmering and by the pilaf and risotto methods.**
6. **Distinguish major kinds and shapes of commercial pasta and determine their quality.**
7. **Prepare fresh and commercial pasta products, and list the steps involved in the alternate steam-table method of its preparation.**

A. Terms

Fill in each blank with the term that is defined or described.

____________________ 1. Rice that is first cooked in fat, then in liquid; braised rice.

____________________ 2. Firm, not soft or mushy; a term often used to describe the doneness of properly cooked pasta.

____________________ 3. A plant that bears seed pods that split along two opposite sides when ripe. Also, the seed from such a plant, used as food.

____________________ 4. A variety of short-grain rice from Italy.

____________________ **5.** Seeds from various types of green beans.

____________________ **6.** An extra-long-grain rice from India, with a distinctive nutty flavor.

____________________ **7.** Mexican whole-grain hominy.

____________________ **8.** A paste made of fresh basil and other ingredients, often used as a pasta sauce.

____________________ **9.** The generic Indian term for dried legume.

____________________ **10.** An Asian sweet-tasting short-grain rice that becomes quite sticky and chewy when cooked, usually by steaming.

____________________ **11.** A granular pasta made from semolina wheat and cooked by soaking and then steaming. This product is often mistaken for a type of grain.

____________________ **12.** A type of cracked wheat that has been partially cooked; often used in salads.

____________________ **13.** An Italian rice dish made by adding stock a little at a time to rice in a pan and stirring constantly while it cooks.

____________________ **14.** Rice with the bran left on.

____________________ **15.** High-gluten flour used for the best-quality commercial macaroni products.

____________________ **16.** Baked casserole made of wide, flat noodles layered with other products such as tomato sauce and cheese.

____________________ **17.** Pillow-shaped stuffed egg noodles.

____________________ **18.** Corn treated with lye and cracked into a coarse meal.

____________________ **19.** An aromatic white rice from Thailand.

____________________ **20.** A thin Japanese noodle made from buckwheat.

____________________ **21.** A lens-shaped legume.

____________________ **22.** The part of a whole grain that is the embryo of a new plant.

____________________ **23.** The starchy mass that forms most of the kernel of a grain.

____________________ **24.** The French location where the most prized green lentils are grown.

____________________ **25.** Seafood product sometimes used to give a black color to pasta.

______________________ **26.** Two names for a wheat-like grain that may be an ancient ancestor of modern wheat.

____

______________________ **27.** Thin noodles made with mung bean starch.

______________________ **28.** Italian cornmeal.

B. Short-Answer Questions

1. Describe the basic cooking procedure for dried kidney beans. Use numbered steps.

____

____

____

____

____

____

____

____

____

2. What is the main difference between the procedure for split peas and the procedure for cooking dried kidney beans? ______________________

____

3. The four main parts of a whole grain are ______________________ , ______________________ , ______________________ , and ______________________ . The part that forms the largest portion of the grain is the ______________________ .

4. Glutinous rice is usually cooked by what cooking method? ______________________ . Before it can be cooked by this method, it must first be ______________________ .

5. What legume has the most high-quality protein? ______

6. What is parboiled rice? ______

______

7. Which kind of rice is most often used as a side dish—short grain, medium grain, or long grain? ______

8. If you are making pilaf with 1 qt (or 1 L) of raw rice, how much stock will you need? ______

9. To cook 1 lb of spaghetti, how much water do you need? ______

10. To get three 10-oz portions (or, if you use metric units, three 300-g portions) of cooked spaghetti, about how much dry, commercial spaghetti do you need? ______

11. What is the purpose of washing white rice before boiling it? ______

______

12. Describe the procedure for preparing or cooking rice noodles for use in stir-fried dishes.

______

______

______

______

C. Pasta Shapes

In the space before the name of each pasta shape, write the letter of the illustration that corresponds.

_______ 1. Fusilli

_______ 2. Ditalini

_______ 3. Spaghettini

_______ 4. Lasagne

_______ 5. Penne

_______ 6. Orzo

_______ 7. Stelline

_______ 8. Ziti

_______ 9. Conchiglie

_______ 10. Elbow macaroni

_______ 11. Fettuccine

_______ 12. Manicotti

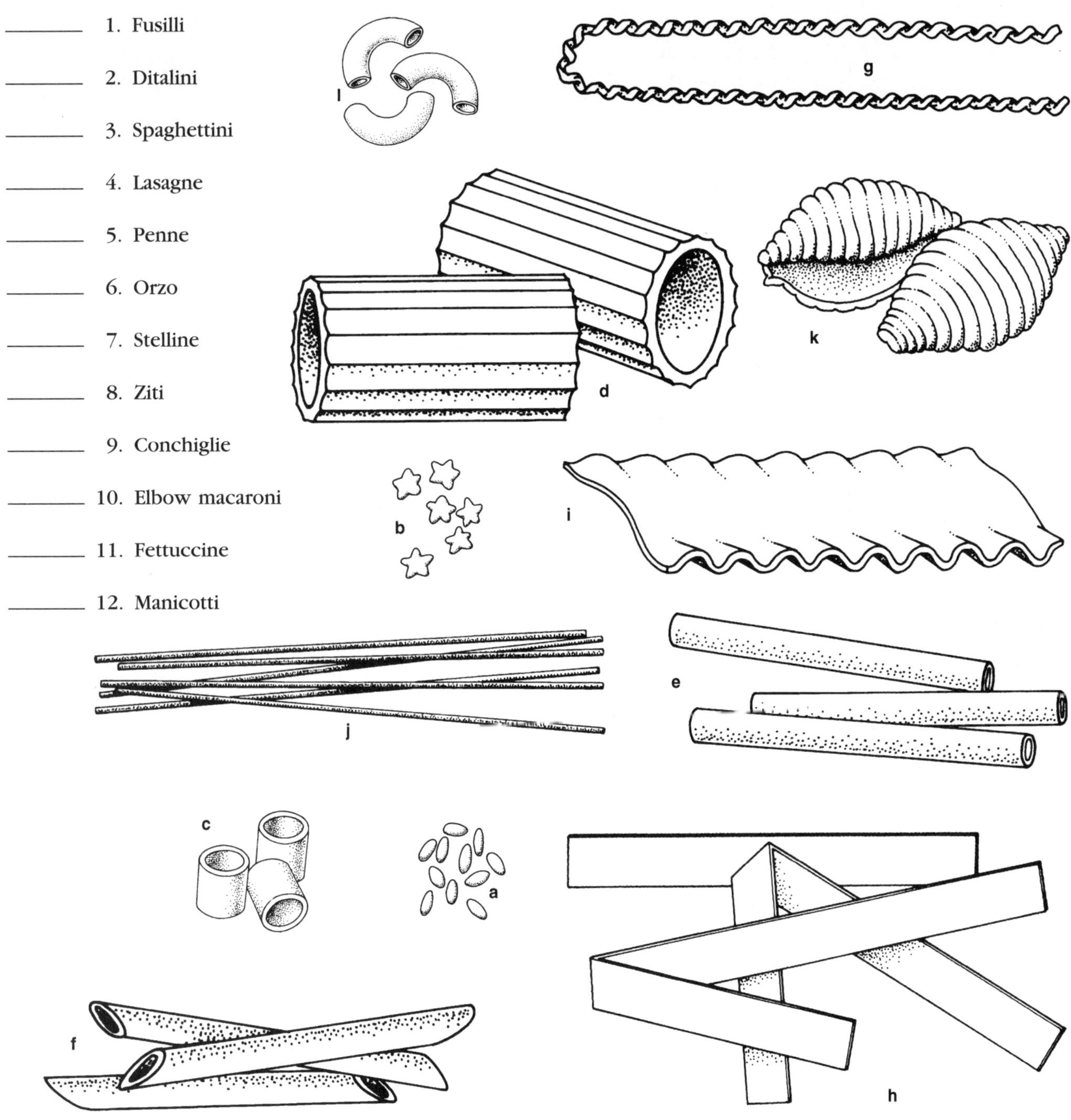

D. Recipe Conversion

The following ingredients and quantities are for a recipe for Pesto, yielding 12 portions at 2 oz each. Convert the recipe to the yields indicated.

	12 portions, 2 oz each	4 portions, 2 oz each	16 portions, 1½ oz each
Fresh basil leaves	2 qt	____________	____________
Olive oil	1½ cups	____________	____________
Pignoli	2 oz	____________	____________
Garlic cloves	6	____________	____________
Salt	1½ tsp	____________	____________
Parmesan cheese	5 oz	____________	____________
Romano cheese	1½ oz	____________	____________

The following ingredients and quantities are for a recipe for Pasta e Fagioli, yielding 12 portions, 8 fl oz each. Convert the recipe to the yields indicated.

	12 portions, 8 fl oz each	16 portions, 8 fl oz each	16 portions, 10 fl oz each
Dried cranberry beans	12 oz	____________	____________
Olive oil	4 fl oz	____________	____________
Pancetta	6 oz	____________	____________
Onion	6 oz	____________	____________
Carrot	6 oz	____________	____________
Celery	6 oz	____________	____________
Fresh sage leaves	4	____________	____________
Fresh rosemary	1 tbsp	____________	____________
Chopped parsley	3 tbsp	____________	____________
Water	2½ qt	____________	____________
Tomato paste	1 oz	____________	____________
Dried fettuccine	1 lb	____________	____________

Recipe Conversion—Metric

The following ingredients and quantities are for a recipe for Pesto, yielding 12 portions at 60 mL each. Convert the recipe to the yields indicated.

	12 portions, 60 mL each	4 portions, 60 mL each	16 portions, 45 mL each
Fresh basil leaves	2 L	________	________
Olive oil	375 mL	________	________
Pignoli	60 g	________	________
Garlic cloves	6	________	________
Salt	7 mL	________	________
Parmesan cheese	150 g	________	________
Romano cheese	45 g	________	________

The following ingredients and quantities are for a recipe for Pasta e Fagioli, yielding 12 portions at 240 mL each. Convert the recipe to the yields indicated.

	12 portions, 240 mL each	16 portions, 240 mL each	16 portions, 300 mL each
Dried cranberry beans	360 g	________	________
Olive oil	120 mL	________	________
Pancetta	180 g	________	________
Onion	180 g	________	________
Carrot	90 g	________	________
Celery	90 g	________	________
Fresh sage leaves	4	________	________
Fresh rosemary	15 mL	________	________
Chopped parsley	45 mL	________	________
Water	2.5 L	________	________
Tomato paste	30 g	________	________
Dried fettuccine	450 g	________	________

E. Portion Cost

Cost out the following recipes. For prices of the ingredients, use figures supplied by your instructor or the *Sample Prices* in the Appendix of this *Study Guide*.

ITEM: **FETTUCCINE ALFREDO**

Ingredient	Recipe Quantity	AP Quantity	Price	Total Amount
Fresh pasta				
Flour	1 lb	________	________	________
Eggs	5	________	________	________
Olive oil	½ oz	________	________	________
Heavy cream	1 pt	________	________	________
Butter	2 oz	________	________	________
Parmesan cheese	6 oz	________	________	________
			Total cost	________
			Number of portions	10
			Cost per portion	________

ITEM: **BULGUR PILAF**

Ingredient	Recipe Quantity	AP Quantity	Price	Total Amount
Butter	1 oz	________	________	________
Onion, chopped fine	4 oz	________	________	________
Bulgur, coarse	8 oz	________	________	________
Chicken stock	1½ pt	________	________	________
			Total cost	________
			Number of portions	12
			Cost per portion	________

Portion Cost—Metric

Cost out the following recipes. For prices of the ingredients, use figures supplied by your instructor or the *Sample Prices* in the Appendix of this *Study Guide*.

ITEM: **FETTUCCINE ALFREDO**

Ingredient	Recipe Quantity	AP Quantity	Price	Total Amount
Fresh pasta				
Flour	450 g	______	______	______
Eggs	5	______	______	______
Olive oil	15 mL	______	______	______
Heavy cream	500 mL	______	______	______
Butter	60 g	______	______	______
Parmesan cheese	175 g	______	______	______
			Total cost	______
			Number of portions	10
			Cost per portion	______

ITEM: **BULGUR PILAF**

Ingredient	Recipe Quantity	AP Quantity	Price	Total Amount
Butter	30 g	______	______	______
Onion, chopped fine	125 g	______	______	______
Bulgur, coarse	250 g	______	______	______
Chicken stock	750 mL	______	______	______
			Total cost	______
			Number of portions	12
			Cost per portion	______

Chapter 20

Cooking for Vegetarian Diets

This chapter gives you the information you need in order to plan recipes and menus suitable for various styles of vegetarian diets.

After studying Chapter 20, you should be able to:

1. **Describe the main types of vegetarian diets.**
2. **Describe complementary proteins and describe how to include them in the diet.**
3. **List three nutrients other than proteins that nonvegetarians get mostly from animal products, and describe how vegetarians can include these nutrients in their diets.**
4. **Name and describe five food types derived from soybeans.**
5. **Explain why refined sugar may not be permitted in a vegan diet.**
6. **List seven guidelines for building a vegetarian menu.**

A. Terms

Fill in each blank with the term that is defined or described.

____________________ 1. A compound or molecule that, when combined with similar compounds, makes up a protein molecule.

____________________ 2. A paste made by fermenting soybeans and various grains.

____________________ 3. A style of vegetarian diet that excludes all animal products.

____________________ 4. A style of vegetarian diet that excludes all animal products except eggs and dairy products.

____________________ 5. A style of vegetarian diet that excludes all animal products except eggs.

____________________ 6. A style of vegetarian diet that excludes all animal products except dairy products.

_____________ 7. A style of vegetarian diet in which fish may be eaten.

_____________ 8. A protein food made from defatted soy flour, processed and dried to give it a spongelike texture, often flavored to taste like meat.

_____________ 9. A liquid product made by soaking dried soybeans, draining them, grinding them, combining them with water and bringing to a boil, and then straining.

_____________ 10. A product made by curdling the item described in number 9.

_____________ 11. A fermented soybean product, originating in Indonesia, with a dense, meaty texture.

_____________ 12. An amino acid that must be included in the diet in order for the body to get adequate protein.

_____________ 13. A protein or protein food that contains all the amino acids described in number 12.

_____________ 14. Protein foods that, when eaten together, supply all the amino acids described in number 12.

B. Short-Answer Questions

1. In addition to protein, what three nutrients, normally found in animal products, must be found in other sources in vegetarian diets and, thus, are of special concern? List as many nonanimal sources of these nutrients as you can.

   Nutrient: _____________

   Sources: _____________

   ____

   Nutrient: _____________

   Sources: _____________

   ____

   Nutrient: _____________

   Sources: _____________

   ____

2. List three categories of foods that are valuable sources of protein in a vegan diet.

   ____

   ____

   ____

3. In addition to the foods listed in question 2, list foods that a lacto-vegetarian can add to his or her diet to supply protein. ______

______

4. Considering the subject of complementary proteins, explain the meaning of "limiting amino acid." ______

______

______

______

5. Combine the following three kinds of foods into three groups that are good sources of complementary proteins:

Whole grains

Dried legumes

Milk products

______

______

______

6. How many amino acids are considered "essential amino acids"? ______

7. Name and describe three types of tofu.

______

______

______

8. Name three plant products that contain complete protein.

______

______

______

9. Why are some sugar products avoided by many vegetarians? ______

______

10. What sugar products can be included in vegetarian diets? ______

______

C. Recipe Conversion

The following ingredients and quantities are for a recipe for Noodle Bowl with Stir-Fried Vegetables, yielding 12 portions, 4 oz noodles and 6 oz vegetables each. Convert the recipe to the yields indicated.

	12 portions, 4 oz noodles each 6 oz vegetables each	**18 portions, 4 oz noodles each 6 oz vegetables each**	**18 portions, 5 oz noodles each 8 oz vegetables each**
Vegetable oil	2 fl oz	________	________
Scallions	4	________	________
Garlic cloves	2	________	________
Chopped ginger root	1 tsp	________	________
Carrots	6 oz	________	________
Red bell peppers	6 oz	________	________
Shiitake mushroom caps	8 oz	________	________
Bok choy	1 lb	________	________
Mung bean sprouts	4 oz	________	________
Snow peas	8 oz	________	________
Firm tofu	1 lb 4 oz	________	________
Roasted peanuts	6 oz	________	________
Soy sauce	3 fl oz	________	________
Hoisin sauce	2 fl oz	________	________
Vegetable stock	4 fl oz	________	________
Sesame oil	1 tbsp	________	________
Cooked Chinese noodles	3 lb	________	________

D. Recipe Conversion—Metric

The following ingredients and quantities are for a recipe for Noodle Bowl with Stir-Fried Vegetables, yielding 12 portions, 125 g noodles and 180 g vegetables each. Convert the recipe to the yields indicated.

	12 portions, 125 g noodles each 180 g vegetables each	18 portions, 125 g noodles each 180 g vegetables each	18 portions, 150 g noodles each 250 g vegetables each
Vegetable oil	60 mL	________	________
Scallions	4	________	________
Garlic cloves	2	________	________
Chopped ginger root	5 mL	________	________
Carrots	180 g	________	________
Red bell peppers	180 g	________	________
Shiitake mushroom caps	250 g	________	________
Bok choy	500 g	________	________
Mung bean sprouts	125 g	________	________
Snow peas	250 g	________	________
Firm tofu	625 g	________	________
Roasted peanuts	180 g	________	________
Soy sauce	90 mL	________	________
Hoisin sauce	60 mL	________	________
Vegetable stock	125 mL	________	________
Sesame oil	15 mL	________	________
Cooked Chinese noodles	1.5 kg	________	________

Chapter 21

Salad Dressings and Salads

Although some of the preparations in this chapter involve cooking, most of our attention is on foods that are served and eaten raw. Emphasis is on product understanding and on careful preparation.

After studying Chapter 21, you should be able to:

1. **Identify the major salad dressing ingredients.**
2. **Prepare the following: oil and vinegar dressings, mayonnaise and mayonnaise-based dressings, cooked dressings, and specialty dressings.**
3. **Identify and describe five different salad types, and select appropriate recipes for use as appetizer, accompaniment, main course, separate course, or dessert salad.**
4. **Identify a dozen popular salad greens, list six categories of other salad ingredients; and recognize several examples from each category.**
5. **Judge the quality of fruits and complete the pre-preparation procedures for fruit.**
6. **Identify the four basic parts of a salad.**
7. **Prepare and arrange salads that achieve maximum eye appeal.**
8. **Set up an efficient system for producing salads in quantity.**
9. **Prepare the following types of salads: green, vegetable, bound, fruit, combination, and gelatin.**
10. **Set up a successful salad bar and buffet service.**

A. Terms

Fill in each blank with the term that is defined or described.

______________________ 1. A red-leafed, Italian variety of chickory.

______________________ 2. A salad mixed with a heavy dressing, such as mayonnaise, to hold it together.

______________________ 3. A famous salad made of romaine lettuce and a dressing made of olive oil, lemon juice, eggs, garlic, and anchovies.

______________________ 4. To soak a food in a seasoned liquid to give it flavor and moistness.

______________________ 5. A dark brown vinegar that has been aged in wooden barrels.

______________________ 6. Oil that has been treated so that it will stay clear and liquid when refrigerated.

______________________ 7. A mixture of tender, baby lettuces.

______________________ 8. A delicate, tender variety of curly endive that is not as bitter as curly endive.

______________________ 9. The best grade of olive oil, made from the first pressing of olives.

______________________ 10. A brand of sheep's-milk cheese made only in a specific region of France.

______________________ 11. A uniform mixture of two unmixable liquids.

______________________ 12. A salad dressing made of oil, vinegar, and seasonings.

______________________ 13. Having a smooth scar on the stem end of a melon, with no trace of stem.

______________________ 14. A classic salad made of apples, celery, and walnuts, with a mayonnaise-based dressing.

______________________ 15. The French name for a small, delicate salad green also known as corn salad, field salad, and lamb's lettuce.

B. True/False

T F 1. Luncheon salads served as a main course must always contain a meat or seafood item.

T F 2. The four basic parts of a salad are the underliner, the base, the lettuce, and the garnish.

T F 3. The dressing should be added to a green salad at least a half hour before service, so that the flavors have time to blend.

T F 4. Cutting ingredients neatly is one way to enhance the appearance of a salad.

T F 5. In general, salad ingredients should be in bite-sized pieces.

T F 6. The purpose of garnish is to make a salad more attractive to the eye.

T F 7. Peaches, pears, and pineapples are examples of fruits that will discolor when cut and exposed to air.

T F 8. Boston lettuce is often tough and bitter, so it is not used by itself in green salads.

T F 9. Watercress is used mainly as a garnish and is inappropriate in mixed green salads.

T F 10. Moisture is necessary to maintain crispness in salad greens.

T F 11. Cooked vegetables to be used in salads must always be cooked until very tender.

T F 12. Raw ingredients should never be added to bound salads.

T F 13. To prevent food-borne disease, the ingredients of a mayonnaise-based salad must be cold when they are combined.

T F 14. Dressings for fruit salads should never be sweetened, so that they will counteract the sweetness of the fruit.

C. Gelatin Review

1. Gelatin dissolves in water at about ______ degrees Fahrenheit (or ______ degrees Celsius).

2. To avoid lumping, plain gelatin is first mixed with ____________________.

3. To use a flavored gelatin sweetened with sugar, you need ______ ounces of gelatin mix per gallon of water (or ______ grams of gelatin mix per liter of water).

4. Basic proportions for unflavored gelatin are ______ ounces of dry gelatin per gallon of liquid (or ______ grams per liter).

5. The setting power of gelatin is weakened by ____________________, by ____________________, and by ____________________. Therefore, most gelatin salads need more gelatin than the basic proportion indicated in number 4.

6. To dissolve sweetened, flavored gelatin, stir it into ____________________ water.

7. ____________________ and ____________________ are two examples of fresh fruits that should not be added to gelatin.

8. The proper time to mix solid ingredients into gelatin is ____

____.

9. In the space below, write out the basic procedure for unmolding gelatin.

____

____

____

____

____

____

____

____

D. Salad Dressing Review

1. The two main ingredients of most standard salad dressings are ____________ and ____________. Other ingredients, such as seasonings, herbs, and egg yolks, are added to modify flavor and texture.

2. ______________________________ is an all-purpose blend of oils that can be used for a wide variety of dressings because of its neutral flavor.

3. Five examples of different vinegars that can be used to make salad dressings are:

   ____

   ____

   ____

   ____

   ____

4. To make a basic oil and vinegar dressing, you need ______ pint(s) of oil for each pint of vinegar.

5. The most important thickening agent in cooked dressing is ____________, while the ingredient that makes mayonnaise thick is ____________.

6. So that the dressing will not be too acidic, a vinegar that contains more than 5% acid may have to be ______________________________ before being included in the dressing.

7. Suggest one ingredient that can be substituted for oil to make a low-fat vinaigrette. ____________

8. In the space below, explain how to make mayonnaise. Be sure to include all necessary steps, and number the steps to make the procedure easier to read. Include ingredient quantities if your instructor asks you to do so.

   ____

   ____

   ____

   ____

E. Math Exercise: Trimming Loss

The exercises below are of two kinds, calculating yield and calculating amount needed. To do the calculations, you need to know the percentage yield for each fruit, as listed in Chapter 21 of the text. For your convenience, the necessary percentages are repeated here.

Apples	75%	Papayas	65%
Bananas	70%	Peaches	75%
Kiwi fruit	80%	Pears	75%
Mangoes	75%	Pineapples	50%
Oranges (sectioned)	65%	Watermelon	45%

Calculating Amount Needed

Assume you need the following quantities, EP (edible portion, with no peels, pits, cores, or stems), of the indicated fresh fruits. Calculate the AP weight you will need to get the required yield. (Questions 1-7 use U.S. measures; questions 8-14 use metric measures. Answer whichever questions are assigned by your instructor.)

	EP Weight Desired	AP Weight Needed
1. Bananas	12 oz	__________
2. Apples	2 lb	__________
3. Peaches	3 lb	__________
4. Oranges (sectioned)	½ lb	__________
5. Kiwi fruit	6 oz	__________
6. Pineapple	8 oz	__________
7. Papaya	1½ lb	__________
8. Bananas	350 g	__________
9. Apples	1 kg	__________
10. Peaches	1.5 kg	__________
11. Oranges (sections)	250 g	__________
12. Kiwi fruit	175 g	__________
13. Pineapple	250 g	__________
14. Papaya	750 g	__________

Calculating Yield

Assume you have the following quantities, AP, of the indicated fresh fruits. Calculate the EP weight you will have left after trimming, peeling, coring, etc. (Questions 15–21 use U.S. measures; questions 22–28 use metric measures. Answer whichever questions are assigned by your instructor.)

	AP Weight	EP Weight
15. Pears	3½ lb	______
16. Bananas	6 lb	______
17. Mangoes	2½ lb	______
18. Watermelon	4½ lb	______
19. Kiwi fruit	1 lb	______
20. Apples	2 lb	______
21. Pineapple	3½ lb	______
22. Pears	1.6 kg	______
23. Bananas	3 kg	______
24. Mangoes	1.2 kg	______
25. Watermelon	2.3 kg	______
26. Kiwi fruit	400 g	______
27. Apples	1 kg	______
28. Pineapple	1.5 kg	______

F. Recipe Conversion

The following ingredients and quantities are for a recipe for Cucumbers and Onions in Sour Cream, yielding 25 salads at 3½ oz each. Convert the recipe to the yields indicated.

	25 portions, 3½ oz each	40 portions, 3½ oz each	14 portions, 3 oz each
Cider vinegar	1 pt	______	______
Water	1 cup	______	______
Sugar	1 oz	______	______
Salt	2 tsp	______	______
White pepper	½ tsp	______	______
Cucumbers, peeled	4 lb	______	______
Onions, peeled	1 lb	______	______
Sour cream	1 pt	______	______
Mayonnaise	1 cup	______	______
Lettuce leaves for underliners*	25	______	______

**Note:* This ingredient is calculated differently from the others. Can you see why?

Recipe Conversion—Metric

The following ingredients and quantities are for a recipe for Cucumbers and Onions in Sour Cream, yielding 25 salads at 100 g each. Convert the recipe to the yields indicated.

	25 portions, 100 g each	40 portions, 100 g each	14 portions, 90 g each
Cider vinegar	500 mL	________	________
Water	250 mL	________	________
Sugar	30 g	________	________
Salt	10 mL	________	________
White pepper	2 mL	________	________
Cucumbers, peeled	2 kg	________	________
Onions, peeled	500 g	________	________
Sour cream	500 mL	________	________
Mayonnaise	250 mL	________	________
Lettuce leaves for underliners*	25	________	________

Note: *Note:* This ingredient is calculated differently from the others. Can you see why?

G. Portion Cost

Cost out the following recipe. For prices of the ingredients, use figures supplied by your instructor or the *Sample Prices* in the Appendix of this *Study Guide*.

ITEM: **CARROT RAISIN SALAD**

Ingredient	Recipe Quantity	AP Quantity	Price	Total Amount
Carrots, AP	5 lb	______	______	______
Raisins	8 oz	______	______	______
Mayonnaise	1½ cups	______	______	______
Salad oil	6 fl oz	______	______	______
Wine vinegar	2 fl oz	______	______	______
Iceberg lettuce	1 head	______	______	______
			Total cost	______
			Number of portions	25
			Cost per portion	______

Portion Cost—Metric

Cost out the following recipe. For prices of the ingredients, use figures supplied by your instructor or the *Sample Prices* in the Appendix of this *Study Guide*.

ITEM: **CARROT RAISIN SALAD**

Ingredient	Recipe Quantity	AP Quantity	Price	Total Amount
Carrots, AP	2 kg	________	________	________
Raisins	200 g	________	________	________
Mayonnaise	300 mL	________	________	________
Salad oil	150 mL	________	________	________
Wine vinegar	50 mL	________	________	________
Iceberg lettuce	1 head	________	________	________
			Total cost	________
			Number of portions	25
			Cost per portion	________

Chapter 22

Sandwiches

Chapters 22 through 27 are a continuation of the pantry unit begun in Chapter 21. This chapter covers the basics of preparing sandwiches of all types. Although sandwich production may seem simple at first glance, it exemplifies many of the basic principles of the professional kitchen, such as careful and thorough mise en place, well-developed manual skills, and efficient planning and organization of tasks.

After studying Chapter 22, you should be able to:

1. **Select, store, and serve fresh, good-quality breads for sandwiches.**
2. **Use sandwich spreads correctly.**
3. **Identify the most popular types of sandwich fillings.**
4. **Set up an efficient sandwich station.**
5. **Prepare the major types of sandwiches to order.**
6. **Prepare sandwiches in quantity.**

A. Terms

Fill in each blank with the term that is defined or described.

____________________ 1. A sandwich made of corned beef, sauerkraut, Swiss cheese, and Russian dressing on rye bread.

____________________ 2. A long, rectangular loaf of bread, often used for sandwiches.

_______________ 3. A sandwich that consists of a filling between two slices of bread.

_______________ 4. A sandwich made of a slice of bread with a topping, but with no top slice of bread.

_______________ 5. A multidecker sandwich made of three slices of toast spread with mayonnaise and filled with sliced chicken or turkey, lettuce, tomato, and bacon.

_______________ 6. A small, fancy sandwich, generally made from light, delicate ingredients and bread that has been trimmed of crusts.

_______________ 7. A thin sheet of bread dough baked with a topping, often but not always including tomatoes and cheese.

_______________ 8. A cold sandwich in which the filling is wrapped in a tortilla or similar thin dough product.

_______________ 9. A hot grilled sandwich usually prepared in equipment that compresses the bread and filling and grills both sides of the sandwich at the same time.

B. Short-Answer Questions

1. List six types of bread that can be used for sandwiches.

   (a) _______________

   (b) _______________

   (c) _______________

   (d) _______________

   (e) _______________

   (f) _______________

2. What are the two most commonly used spreads for sandwiches?

   ____

   ____

3. The following are some basic categories of sandwich filling ingredients. Fill in the blanks with specific examples of each group, naming as many examples as there are spaces.

Beef

(a) ____________________

(b) ____________________

(c) ____________________

(d) ____________________

(e) ____________________

(f) ____________________

Pork and sausage products

(a) ____________________

(b) ____________________

(c) ____________________

(d) ____________________

(e) ____________________

(f) ____________________

(g) ____________________

Poultry

(a) ____________________

(b) ____________________

Fish and shellfish

(a) ____________________

(b) ____________________

(c) ____________________

(d) ____________________

Cheese

(a) ______________________________

(b) ______________________________

(c) ______________________________

(d) ______________________________

(e) ______________________________

4. List four basic hand tools that are essential on a short-order sandwich station.

(a) ______________________________

(b) ______________________________

(c) ______________________________

(d) ______________________________

5. In the space below, draw a diagram of the proper way to cut a club sandwich.

6. Suppose you are assigned to make a large quantity of turkey sandwiches, using mayonnaise as the spread and lettuce leaves and sliced turkey breast as the filling. In the space below, write out the procedure you would use to prepare the sandwiches efficiently and quickly. Be sure to include all the steps, and number the steps to make the procedure easier to read.

7. Two of the most basic and classic Italian pizzas are called Margherita and Marinara. List the toppings for these two pizzas.

Margherita: ______________________________

Marinara: ______________________________

8. What technique is used to make a grilled panino sandwich if a panino press is not available?

____

____

C. Recipe Conversion

The following ingredients and quantities are for Chili Marinade for Grilled Salmon Sandwiches. Convert the recipe to the yields indicated.

	6 oz	16 oz	40 oz
Chili powder	2 oz	________	________
Dried oregano	1 tbsp	________	________
Ground cloves	½ tsp	________	________
Garlic, crushed	1 oz	________	________
Salt	2 tsp	________	________
Brown sugar	1 oz	________	________
Red wine vinegar	4 fl oz	________	________

Recipe Conversion—Metric

The following ingredients and quantities are for Chili Marinade for Grilled Salmon Sandwiches. Convert the recipe to the yields indicated.

	180	500 g	1.25 kg
Chili powder	60 g	________	________
Dried oregano	15 mL	________	________
Ground cloves	2 mL	________	________
Garlic, crushed	30 g	________	________
Salt	10 mL	________	________
Brown sugar	30 g	________	________
Red wine vinegar	120 mL	________	________

Chapter 23

Hors d'Oeuvres

Because there are so many kinds of hors d'oeuvres, using all types of meats, poultry, fish, vegetables, and starch products, in this chapter you will use all the skills you have learned in earlier chapters.

After studying Chapter 23, you should be able to:

1. **Name and describe the two principal methods of serving hors d'oeuvres at a reception.**
2. **Prepare canapés.**
3. **Prepare hors d'oeuvres cocktails and relishes.**
4. **Prepare dips.**
5. **Prepare a variety of other hors d'oeuvres, including antipasti, bruschette, and tapas.**
6. **Name and describe the three types of sturgeon caviar, and name and describe three other kinds of caviar.**

A. Terms

Fill in each blank with the term that is defined or described.

______________________ 1. A bite-sized, open-faced sandwich, served as an hors d'oeuvre.

______________________ 2. French term for raw vegetables, served as hors d'oeuvres.

______________________ 3. A category of hors d'oeuvres that includes raw vegetables (as in number 2) and pickled items.

______________________ 4. A Mexican-style dip made of mashed avocado.

______________________ 5. A category of appetizer that includes various seafoods or fruits, served cold, usually with a tart or tangy sauce.

______________________ 6. An Italian hors d'oeuvre.

______________________ 7. A small appetizer offered, compliments of the chef, to guests seated at their tables, either before or after they have ordered from the menu.

______________________ 8. Italian-style garlic toast, usually served with toppings. Similar to large canapés.

______________________ 9. Salted sturgeon eggs.

______________________ 10. Spanish-style hors d'oeuvre, usually served on a small plate and intended to be eaten with wine or other drinks.

B. Hors d'Oeuvre Review

1. The three basic parts of a canapé are ______________, ______________, and ______________.

2. In the space below, draw diagrams of three different ways that bread slices can be cut into various shapes for canapés.

3. List four different items that can be used as bases for canapés.

   (a) ______________

   (b) ______________

   (c) ______________

   (d) ______________

4. What are the two most common types of spreads used for canapés?

   ____

   ____

5. The following are some basic categories of canapé garnishes. Fill in the blanks with specific examples of each group, naming as many examples as there are spaces.

Fish and shellfish products

(a) ______________________

(b) ______________________

(c) ______________________

(d) ______________________

(e) ______________________

(f) ______________________

(g) ______________________

(h) ______________________

Vegetables, pickles, and relishes

(a) ______________________

(b) ______________________

(c) ______________________

(d) ______________________

(e) ______________________

(f) ______________________

(g) ______________________

(h) ______________________

(i) ______________________

(j) ______________________

Meats

(a) ______________________

(b) ______________________

(c) ______________________

(d) ______________________

6. The two primary methods of serving hors d'oeuvres are ____________________ and ____________________.

7. When raw oysters are served as a seafood cocktail, the best way to keep them cold is ______________________________.

8. When hot items are served on an hors d'oeuvre buffet, the best way to keep them hot is ______________________________.

9. Describe the proper consistency for dips. ______________________________

10. Describe the procedure for making a basic bruschetta. ______________________________

11. The three categories of caviar, ranging from the largest to the smallest, are ______________, ______________, and ______________.

12. Caviar made with a relatively low proportion of salt is called ______________________________.

13. Proper serving temperature for caviar is ______________________________.

C. Recipe Conversion

The following ingredients and quantities are for a Clam Dip recipe that yields 1 qt. Convert the recipe to the yields indicated.

	1 qt	**1½ pt**	**1 gal**
Cream cheese	1 lb 4 oz	______	______
Clam juice	3 oz	______	______
Dijon-style mustard	2 oz	______	______
Worcestershire sauce	1 oz	______	______
Horseradish	1 tsp	______	______
Grated onion	1½ oz	______	______
Hot pepper sauce	½ tsp	______	______
Canned clams, drained	12 oz	______	______
Salt	to taste	______	______
White pepper	to taste	______	______

Recipe Conversion—Metric

The following ingredients and quantities are for a Clam Dip recipe that yields 1 L. Convert the recipe to the yields indicated.

	1 L	750 mL	4 L
Cream cheese	625 g	______	______
Clam juice	90 g	______	______
Dijon-style mustard	60 g	______	______
Worcestershire sauce	30 mL	______	______
Horseradish	5 mL	______	______
Grated onion	45 g	______	______
Hot pepper sauce	2 ml	______	______
Canned clams, drained	375 g	______	______
Salt	to taste	______	______
White pepper	to taste	______	______

Chapter 24

Breakfast Preparation

This chapter discusses cooking techniques for breakfast items, illustrated by a few typical recipes. In addition, there is important product information about eggs.

After studying Chapter 24, you should be able to:

1. **Describe the composition of eggs and the major differences among grades.**
2. **Store eggs properly.**
3. **Prepare the following egg items: hard-, medium-, and soft-cooked eggs; poached eggs; fried eggs; baked eggs; scrambled eggs; omelets; entrée soufflés; and savory custards.**
4. **List the key differences between waffle batter and pancake batter, and prepare each.**
5. **Prepare French toast, and identify the common variations possible by changing the basic ingredients.**
6. **Prepare each of the two general types of cooked breakfast cereals.**
7. **Identify the three most common breakfast meats and prepare them.**

A. Terms

Fill in each blank with the term that is defined or described.

_______________ 1. A dish consisting of poached eggs and Canadian bacon on English muffins, coated with Hollandaise sauce.

_______________ 2. Term used to describe fried eggs cooked on one side only.

_______________ 3. An egg baked in an individual serving dish, with or without additional ingredients; resembles a fried egg in appearance.

_______________ 4. A flat, unfolded omelet, consisting of beaten eggs mixed with other ingredients.

_______________ 5. A savory tart consisting of a custard mixture and other ingredients baked in a pastry shell.

_____________ 6. Bread dipped into an egg mixture and cooked on a griddle or in a fry pan or deep-fryer.

_____________ 7. A liquid that is thickened or set by the coagulation of egg protein.

_____________ 8. A thin pancake made without any leavening.

_____________ 9. A food-borne disease that may be spread by contaminated eggs.

B. True/False: Egg and Breakfast Review

T F 1. Fresh or high-grade raw eggs are firmer (less runny) than old or low-grade eggs.

T F 2. The highest Canadian grade for fresh eggs is grade A.

T F 3. One extra-large shell egg weighs slightly more than 2 oz (including the shell).

T F 4. Egg yolks are high in fat.

T F 5. The green color sometimes seen in eggs is due to overcooking.

T F 6. A custard mixture must be heated to the boiling point of water (212°F/100°C) so that it will set properly.

T F 7. Egg whites whip better and make a richer foam if the bowl is lightly greased before breaking the eggs into it.

T F 8. Hard-cooked eggs will be tough and rubbery unless they are cooked long enough to be tenderized.

T F 9. To make soft-cooked eggs, shell eggs are boiled for 5 to 7 minutes.

T F 10. The air sac is located at the small end of the egg.

T F 11. A pinch of cream of tartar improves the foaming ability of egg whites.

T F 12. Making a true French omelet requires high heat.

T F 13. A standard spinach soufflé is made from a thick white sauce, egg yolks, chopped cooked spinach (and sometimes other ingredients for flavoring), plus whipped egg whites folded in just before baking.

T F 14. Waffle batter is usually thinner than pancake batter.

T F 15. Pancake batter should be beaten well to develop a smooth texture.

T F 16. The best way to prepare a large quantity of bacon is to cook it in the deep-fryer.

T F 17. Egg substitutes used for making scrambled eggs contain real egg whites but not yolks.

T F 18. Egg shells are porous, so whole shell eggs can absorb foreign odors when in storage.

T F 19. Sugar whipped into egg whites make an egg white foam more stable.

C. Recipe Conversion

The following ingredients and quantities are for a vegetable frittata recipe that yields 4 portions at 8 oz each. Convert the recipe to the yields indicated.

	4 portions, 8 oz each	10 portions, 8 oz each	10 portions, 6 oz each
Leeks	4 oz	____________	____________
Zucchini	10 oz	____________	____________
Butter	1½ oz	____________	____________
Spinach leaves	8 oz	____________	____________
Eggs, beaten	10 fl oz	____________	____________

Recipe Conversion—Metric

The following ingredients and quantities are a vegetable frittata recipe that yields 4 portions at 240 g each. Convert the recipe to the yields indicated.

	4 portions, 240 g each	10 portions, 240 g each	10 portions, 180 g each
Leeks	4 oz	____________	____________
Zucchini	10 oz	____________	____________
Butter	1½ oz	____________	____________
Spinach leaves	8 oz	____________	____________
Eggs, beaten	10 fl oz	____________	____________

Chapter 25

Dairy and Beverages

Much of this chapter consists of important product information. Here you learn to identify the major types of milk, cream, butter, and cheese products and to cook with them using proper techniques. In addition, you learn about the preparation of coffee and tea beverages.

After studying Chapter 25, you should be able to:

1. **Describe the major milk, cream, and butter products.**
2. **Explain why milk curdles and why it scorches, and identify the steps to take to prevent curdling and scorching.**
3. **Whip cream.**
4. **Describe the most important kinds of cheese used in the kitchen.**
5. **Store and serve cheese properly.**
6. **Cook with cheese.**
7. **Prepare coffee and tea.**

A. Terms

Fill in each blank with the term that is defined or described.

_______________ 1. Milk that has been processed so that the cream doesn't separate out.

_______________ 2. Generic term for cheese made with goats' milk.

_______________ 3. A manufactured product made of fats and other ingredients, intended to resemble butter.

_______________ 4. A dish made of cheddar-type cheese melted with beer and seasonings.

_______________ 5. Milk that has been heat-treated to kill disease-causing bacteria.

_______________ 6. Milk that has not been heat-treated as in number 5.

_______________ 7. A process by which milk proteins coagulate and separate from the whey; in cooking this process is usually undesirable.

_______________ 8. A strong, dark coffee made from beans roasted until they are almost black.

_______________ 9. Tea that has been fermented by allowing the freshly harvested leaves to oxidize in a damp place.

_______________ 10. Tea that has been dried without the fermenting procedure described in number 9.

_______________ 11. Tea that has been only partially fermented, so that it has a greenish-brown color.

_______________ 12. A term meaning "half-cup," referring to strong, dark coffee served in small cups after dinner.

_______________ 13. A dish consisting of Swiss cheeses melted with white wine and served with bread cubes for dipping.

_______________ 14. A slightly aged, cultured heavy cream, often used for sauce-making.

_______________ 15. Cheese that is made with milk from the farmer's own herd or flock on the farm where the animals are raised.

_______________ 16. Cheese that is produced primarily by hand, in small batches, with particular attention to the cheesemaker's art and using as little mechanization as possible.

_______________ 17. A drink made of equal parts espresso and frothy, steamed milk.

_______________ 18. A drink made of espresso and hot chocolate or cocoa.

_______________ 19. A drink made of espresso and steamed milk, using at least twice as much milk as coffee.

_______________ 20. A sweetened blend of tea and hot, spiced milk.

B. Dairy and Cheese Review I

1. In the blanks provided, write in the name of the milk or cream products described.

(a) ______________________ Fresh, liquid, skim milk that has been cultured by bacteria.

(b) ______________________ Milk that has had about 60% of its water content removed.

(c) ______________________ Skim milk that has been dried to a powder.

(d) ______________________ Milk produced by disease-free herds under strict sanitary conditions.

(e) ______________________ Milk that has not been pasteurized.

(f) ______________________ Cream that has been fermented by certain bacteria to make it thick.

(g) ______________________ Sweetened milk with more than half its moisture removed.

(h) ______________________ Milk with all or nearly all its fat removed.

(i) ______________________ Milk with added vitamins.

(j) ______________________ Milk that has been processed at a higher temperature to make it shelf-stable until opened.

2. In the blanks provided, write in the fat content (in percent) of each of the following milk and cream products.

(a) ________% Heavy whipping cream

(b) ________% Whole milk

(c) ________% Half-and-half

(d) ________% Skim milk

(e) ________% Butter

(f) ________% Light cream

3. What is yogurt? ____

____

4. Name four conditions or substances that can make milk curdle.

(a) ____

(b) ____

(c) ____

(d) ____

5. In order to be in the best condition for whipping, heavy cream should be at about what temperature?

____

6. Describe the appearance of properly whipped cream. What happens if the cream is whipped too much?

____

____

____

7. What is the highest Canadian grade of butter? _______

8. What does the term "ripen" mean when referring to cheese?

____

____

____

9. Cheeses can be classified according to how and if they are ripened. List the five categories, and give an example of each kind of cheese.

(a) _______________ Example: _______________

(b) _______________ Example: _______________

(c) _______________ Example: _______________

(d) _______________ Example: _______________

(e) _______________ Example: _______________

10. The label on a package of soft cheese indicates a net weight of 8 oz (227 g) and a fat content of 75%. What is the total weight of the fat in the cheese? Explain your answer. (Caution: This may be a trick question.)

____

____

____

11. What is the proper serving temperature for most cheeses?

____

C. Cheese Review II

The left column below lists the names of various cheeses. The column on the right lists various categories or kinds of cheese. In the space before the name of each cheese, write the letter corresponding to the kind of cheese it is.

_______	**1.** Cheddar	**a.** Unripened
_______	**2.** Roquefort	**b.** Semisoft
_______	**3.** Boucheron	**c.** Soft ripened
_______	**4.** Brie	**d.** Hard ripened
_______	**5.** Limburger	**e.** Blue-veined
_______	**6.** Parmesan	**f.** Goat cheese
_______	**7.** Emmenthaler	**g.** Hard grating (grana)
_______	**8.** American	**h.** Process
_______	**9.** Stilton	
_______	**10.** Port Salut	
_______	**11.** Mozzarella	
_______	**12.** Gorgonzola	
_______	**13.** Romano	
_______	**14.** Fontina	
_______	**15.** Ricotta	
_______	**16.** Liederkranz	
_______	**17.** Cottage	
_______	**18.** Camembert	
_______	**19.** Bel Paese	
_______	**20.** Montrachet	

D. Recipe Conversion

The following ingredients and quantities are for a Welsh Rabbit recipe that yields 25 portions at 4 oz each. Convert the recipe to the yields indicated.

	25 portions, 4 oz each	**4 portions, 4 oz each**	**16 portions, 3 oz each**
Worcestershire sauce	3 tbsp	__________	__________
Dry mustard	2 tsp	__________	__________
Cayenne	pinch	__________	__________
Beer	2½ cups	__________	__________
Cheddar cheese	5 lb	__________	__________
White bread*	25 slices	__________	__________

**Note:* This ingredient is calculated differently from the others.

Recipe Conversion—Metric

The following ingredients and quantities are for a Welsh Rabbit recipe that yields 25 portions at 125 g each. Convert the recipe to the yields indicated.

	25 portions, 125 g each	**4 portions, 125 g each**	**16 portions, 100 g each**
Worcestershire sauce	45 mL	__________	__________
Dry mustard	10 mL	__________	__________
Cayenne	pinch	__________	__________
Beer	625 mL	__________	__________
Cheddar cheese	2.5 kg	__________	__________
White bread*	25 slices	__________	__________

**Note:* This ingredient is calculated differently from the others.

E. Portion Cost

Cost out the following recipe. For prices of the ingredients, use figures supplied by your instructor or the *Sample Prices* in the Appendix of this *Study Guide*.

***ITEM:* CHEESE TART**

Ingredient	Recipe Quantity	AP Quantity	Price	Total Amount
Flour	2 lb	______	______	______
Shortening	1 lb 4 oz	______	______	______
Salt	1½ oz	______	______	______
Water	8 oz	______	______	______
Gruyère cheese	2 lb	______	______	______
Eggs	24	______	______	______
Heavy cream	1 qt	______	______	______
Milk	2 qt	______	______	______
Salt	½ oz	______	______	______
			Total cost	______
			Number of portions	48
			Cost per portion	______

Portion Cost—Metric

Cost out the following recipe. For prices of the ingredients, use figures supplied by your instructor or the *Sample Prices* in the Appendix of this *Study Guide*.

ITEM: **CHEESE TART**

Ingredient	Recipe Quantity	AP Quantity	Price	Total Amount
Flour	1 kg	______	______	______
Shortening	625 g	______	______	______
Salt	15 g	______	______	______
Water	250 mL	______	______	______
Gruyère cheese	1 kg	______	______	______
Eggs	24	______	______	______
Heavy cream	1 L	______	______	______
Milk	2 L	______	______	______
Salt	15 g	______	______	______
			Total cost	______
			Number of portions	48
			Cost per portion	______

Chapter 26

Sausages and Cured Foods

This chapter introduces the specialized subjects of curing, smoking, and sausage-making. This material is part of the general study of garde manger, which you first read about in Chapter 21, Salad Dressings and Salads. There is a great deal of technical information in this chapter, much of which affects food safety, so it is important to study it thoroughly before producing any of the recipes here.

After studying Chapter 26, you should be able to:

1. **Prepare simple dry-cured and brine-cured foods.**
2. **Prepare simple smoked foods.**
3. **Prepare fresh, cured, and smoked sausages.**

A. Terms

Fill in each blank with the term that is defined or described.

____________________ 1. A curing method in which the curing ingredients are packed or rubbed over the food.

____________________ 2. A curing method in which the food is immersed in a solution of the curing ingredients dissolved in water.

____________________ 3. A spice mixture used in some sausages and other meat products. The name means "4 spices."

____________________ 4. A sausage that contains no nitrates or nitrites.

____________________ 5. An artificial but edible sausage casing made of animal connective tissue.

____________________ 6. A smoking method in which the foods are smoked at a high enough temperature to cook them partially or completely.

____________________ 7. The curing agent or chemical in Prague Powder #1, or curing salt.

_______________ **8.** A cancer-causing chemical formed when meat containing nitrates is subjected to very high heat.

_______________ **9.** A sausage grind in which the meat and fat are ground very smooth with the addition of ice or water.

_______________ **10.** The art of making prepared and cooked meat products, especially pork products such as sausages and pâtés.

_______________ **11.** A sausage casing made from animal intestine.

_______________ **12.** A medium-sized casing, about 1 to 1½ inches (3 to 4 cm) in diameter, used for such popular sausages as bratwurst and Italian sausage.

_______________ **13.** A smoking method in which the temperature is kept low so that the smoked food remains uncooked.

_______________ **14.** A patty of sausage meat wrapped in caul.

B. Review of Curing and Smoking

1. The most important ingredient for curing any food, including cured fish, is _______________. This ingredient has two main effects, both of which make the food less hospitable to bacteria:

(a) _______________

_______________ and

(b) _______________

_______________.

2. Curing salt consists of _______________ and _______________, plus coloring to give it a _______________ color. The purpose of the coloring agent is _______________.

3. Two other names for curing salt are _______________ and _______________.

4. The two basic types of cures are _______________ and _______________.

5. Of the two types of cures in question 4, which is most often used for curing whole poultry? _______________

6. What is the main reason for curing all meats, poultry, and fish before smoking them?

____

____

____

7. When cold-smoking food, you should keep the temperature inside the smokehouse to _______________ or lower.

8. A smokehouse consists of four main elements:

a. ______________________________

b. ______________________________

c. ______________________________

d. ______________________________

9. The smoking process consists of three main steps:

a. ______________________________

b. ______________________________

c. ______________________________

C. Review of Sausage-Making

1. The four basic components of fresh sausage meat are ______________, ______________, ______________, and ______________.

2. When extra fat must be added to pork sausage meat, what is the most desirable fat to use? ______________

3. To increase the moisture content of low-fat sausage, you can add ______________ because they help retain moisture.

4. Describe how to prepare natural sausage casings for stuffing.

____

____

____

____

____

____

5. The two basic types of grinds used in the production of sausages are ______________ and ______________. Briefly describe the differences between these two grinding procedures.

____

____

____

____

____

____

____

6. Why must sausage meat be kept very cold during grinding and stuffing?

____

____

D. Recipe Conversion

The following ingredients and quantities are for an Italian sausage recipe that yields 6 lb. Convert the recipe to the yields indicated.

	6 lb	2 lb	15 lb
Lean pork	4 lb 8 oz	________	________
Pork fatback	1 lb 8 oz	________	________
Salt	2 tbsp	________	________
Black pepper	2 tsp	________	________
Fennel seeds	1 tbsp	________	________
Paprika	5 tsp	________	________
Crushed red pepper	1 tsp	________	________
Sugar	2 tsp	________	________
Cold water	6 oz	________	________

E. Recipe Conversion—Metric

The following ingredients and quantities are for an Italian sausage recipe that yields 3 kg. Convert the recipe to the yields indicated.

	3 kg	1 kg	7.5 kg
Lean pork	2250 g	______	______
Pork fatback	750 g	______	______
Salt	30 g	______	______
Black pepper	10 mL	______	______
Fennel seeds	15 mL	______	______
Paprika	25 mL	______	______
Crushed red pepper	5 mL	______	______
Sugar	10 mL	______	______
Cold water	200 mL	______	______

Chapter 27

Pâtés, Terrines, and Other Cold Foods

Your study of garde manger continues with an introduction to the production of pâtés and terrines. These products are not only some of the most important items on the classic cold buffet (which you will read more about in Chapter 28), but they are also served as appetizers on restaurant menus.

After studying Chapter 27, you should be able to:

1. **Prepare and use aspic jellies.**
2. **Prepare and use classic chaud-froid and mayonnaise chaud-froid.**
3. **Prepare livers for use in forcemeats.**
4. **Prepare basic meat and poultry forcemeats.**
5. **Prepare pâtés and terrines using basic forcemeats.**
6. **Prepare galantines.**
7. **Prepare mousseline forcemeats and make terrines based on them.**
8. **Prepare specialty terrines and other molded dishes based on aspics and mousses.**
9. **Handle raw foie gras and prepare foie gras terrines.**
10. **Prepare baked liver terrines.**
11. **Prepare rillettes.**

A. Terms

Fill in each blank with the term that is defined or described.

________________________ **1.** Liver of specially fattened ducks and geese.

________________________ **2.** A forcemeat made of puréed meat, poultry, or fish, heavy cream, and, usually, egg whites.

_______________ 3. The department of a kitchen in which cold foods, including salads and buffet items, are prepared.

_______________ 4. A clarified stock that contains enough gelatin so that it solidifies when cold.

_______________ 5. Unflavored gelatin mixed with a powdered stock base.

_______________ 6. A seasoned mixture of ground meats and other foods, used as a filling or stuffing or as a base for terrines and pâtés.

_______________ 7. Dough or pastry used to make pâtés.

_______________ 8. An opaque, usually white, sauce containing gelatin, used to coat certain cold foods for decorative purposes.

_______________ 9. A seasoned mixture of cooked meat and fat, mashed to a paste; used as an appetizer.

_______________ 10. A creamy, puréed food made light by the addition of whipped cream; often contains gelatin.

_______________ 11. A dish made of a baked forcemeat, usually in a crust.

_______________ 12. A dish similar to that described in number 11, except made without a crust; traditionally baked in an earthenware mold.

_______________ 13. A special type of the item described in number 11, characterized by a coarse texture.

_______________ 14. A forcemeat wrapped in the skin of the animal from which it is made, such as chicken or duck, or rolled into a cylinder without the skin.

B. Review of Aspic and Chaud-Froid Procedures

1. In the space below, write the three basic steps for making a classic aspic jelly.

____

____

____

____

____

____

2. In the space below, write the steps in the general procedure for making a cooled, liquid aspic jelly for coating a food item. Start with cold, solidified aspic jelly.

3. In the space below, write the steps in the general procedure for coating foods with aspic jelly.

4. In the space below, write the ingredients and the procedure for making mayonnaise chaud-froid.

5. In the space below, write the procedure for coating a mold with a uniform layer of aspic jelly.

C. Short-Answer Questions

1. It is especially important to be aware of safe, sanitary food handling when preparing cold foods such as pâtés because ____ ____ ____ ____.

2. The procedure for making a classic aspic jelly is similar to the procedure for making what kind of soup? ____________________

3. Three ingredients that can be included with the regular bones when making stock to help increase the gelatin content are ____________________, ____________________, and ____________________.

4. Mayonnaise chaud-froid is made from two ingredients, ____________________ and ____________________.

5. Classical chaud-froid can be made by adding a liaison to ____________________.

6. Three examples of classic pâté garnish are ____________________, ____________________, and ____________________.

7. A gratin forcemeat is similar to a straight forcemeat, except that some of the meat is ____________________. This type of forcemeat contains a starch binder called a ____________________.

8. In addition to pork and pork fat, a country-style forcemeat usually contains some ____________________.

9. Basic-grind sausage meat is similar to which of the three basic forcemeat types discussed in this chapter? ____________________

10. The most important meat used in the production of pâtés and terrines is ____________________.

11. A basic straight forcemeat is made of ____________________ percent meat and ____________________ percent fat.

12. In five steps, write the procedure for preparing poultry livers for use in forcemeats.

a. ______________________________

b. ______________________________

c. ______________________________

d. ______________________________

e. ______________________________

13. In simplest terms, a terrine is a baked ______________.

14. After a pâté en croûte has baked and cooled, the next step is to pour ______________ through the steam vent holes in order to fill up the space between the crust and the forcemeat, which has shrunk during baking.

15. A mousseline forcemeat is made of puréed meat, poultry, or fish, ______________, and usually egg whites.

16. The four basic steps in making a savory mousse are:

a. ______________________________

b. ______________________________

c. ______________________________

d. ______________________________

17. A raw foie gras should be at what temperature before being deveined? ______________ .

18. When cooking foie gras, it is very important to avoid overcooking because ______________

____

______________________________ .

Chapter 28

Food Presentation and Garnish

This chapter concerns itself with the appearance of food rather than with cooking techniques. The material is meant to be studied not for its own sake but for its application to the food preparations that you learn in the rest of your studies. While it may seem very theoretical at first, it has many practical uses.

After studying Chapter 28, you should be able to:

1. **Explain why attractive food presentation is important.**
2. **Serve food that is attractively arranged on the plate or platter, with proper balance of color, shape, and texture.**
3. **Identify common terms from classical garniture that are still in general use today.**
4. **Garnish a banquet platter with attractive and appropriate vegetable accompaniments.**
5. **Plan and arrange attractive food platters for buffets.**

A. Terms

Fill in each blank with the term that is defined or described.

____________________ 1. To add an edible decorative item to food.

____________________ 2. A decorative edible item added to food.

____________________ 3. A type of buffet serving only appetizers, usually to accompany drinks.

________________ **4.** The centerpiece of a cold buffet platter.

________________ **5.** An oval relish dish.

________________ **6.** Bread slices cut into triangles or heart shapes, toasted, and used as garnish.

________________ **7.** The four components that make up a plated food arrangement.

____

____

____

B. Garnish Review

In the blanks provided, write the specific food items or ingredients that the garnish terms refer to.

________________ **1.** Niçoise

________________ **2.** Dubarry

________________ **3.** Lyonnaise

________________ **4.** Parmentier

________________ **5.** Printanière

________________ **6.** Judic

________________ **7.** Primeurs

________________ **8.** Florentine

________________ **9.** Princesse

________________ **10.** Bouquetière

________________ **11.** Doria

________________ **12.** Jardinière

________________ **13.** Vichy

________________ **14.** Forestière

________________ **15.** Crécy

________________ **16.** Fermière

________________ **17.** Clamart

________________ **18.** Provençale

C. True/False

T F 1. The main meat or fish item on a plate is always placed in the center.

T F 2. The term garnish sometimes refers to vegetable accompaniments.

T F 3. A T-bone steak should be plated so that the bone is toward the back of the plate, away from the customer.

T F 4. To make the portions look generous, the meat and vegetable items on a plate should be piled up against each other.

T F 5. Every buffet platter requires a centerpiece.

T F 6. Filet mignon plated with various garnishes is listed on the menu as "filet mignon with garni."

T F 7. A simple garnish should always be edible, even if it is not intended to be eaten.

T F 8. Deep-fried foods are usually not suited for chafing-dish service.

T F 9. On a buffet, sauces and dressings should be placed next to the items with which they are to be eaten.

D. Review of Cold Platter Design

Following the principles outlined on pages 887–889 of the text, draw diagrams of food arrangements on each of the four platters outlined below. Develop your own designs; do not copy the examples in Figure 28.1. In the blanks provided, you may indicate what foods you are using. Use your ideas, or whatever food items are assigned by your instructor. (A platter may have more than one main food item and/or more than one garnish; for example, slices of veal pâté and slices of pickled veal tongue as two main items on one platter.)

Centerpiece ____________________

Main item(s) ____________________

____

Garnish(es) ____________________

____

Centerpiece ____________________

Main item(s) ____________________

____

Garnish(es) ____________________

____

Centerpiece ____________________

Main item(s) ____________________

____

Garnish(es) ____________________

____

Centerpiece ______________________

Main item(s) ______________________

____

Garnish(es) ______________________

____

Chapter 29

Bakeshop Production: Basic Principles and Ingredients

This is the first of seven chapters dealing with the bakeshop. We begin with some basic principles and an introduction to the primary ingredients used in baking. You will need to understand this material before proceeding to the production chapters.

After studying Chapter 29, you should be able to:

1. **Explain why it is important to weigh baking ingredients.**
2. **Use a baker's balance scale.**
3. **Calculate formulas based on baker's percentages.**
4. **Explain the factors that control the development of gluten in baked products.**
5. **Explain the changes that take place in a dough or batter as it bakes.**
6. **Prevent or retard the staling of baked items.**
7. **Describe the major ingredients of baked goods and their functions and characteristics.**

A. Terms

Fill in each blank with the term that is defined or described.

____________________ 1. The chemical name for regular refined sugar or table sugar.

____________________ 2. A flavoring ingredient consisting of flavorful oils mixed with water with the aid of vegetable gums or other substances.

_______________ 3. A substance, made up of proteins present in wheat flour, that gives structure and strength to baked goods.

_______________ 4. Flour with a high protein content, derived from hard wheat.

_______________ 5. Flour with a low protein content, from soft wheat.

_______________ 6. The process by which yeast changes carbohydrates to alcohol and carbon dioxide gas.

_______________ 7. The primary sugar present in corn syrup.

_______________ 8. The rendered fat of hogs.

_______________ 9. The change in texture of baked goods due in part to the loss of moisture by the starch granules.

_______________ 10. A flavoring ingredient consisting of flavorful oils and other substances dissolved in alcohol.

_______________ 11. The product that results when cocoa beans are roasted and ground.

_______________ 12. The white or yellowish fat that is a component of the product described in number 11.

_______________ 13. The dry powder that remains after part of the fat is removed from the product described in number 11.

_______________ 14. The dried powder as described in number 13, but processed with alkali.

_______________ 15. The product that is made when sugar is added to the product described in number 11.

_______________ 16. The product that is made when sugar and milk solids are added to the product described in number 11.

_______________ 17. The production or incorporation of gases in a baked product to increase volume and to produce shape and texture.

_______________ 18. Any of a group of solid fats, usually white and tasteless, that have been especially formulated for baking.

_______________ 19. The process of beating fat and sugar together to incorporate air.

_______________ 20. The process of whipping eggs, with or without sugar, to incorporate air.

_______________ 21. The finest or smoothest variety of confectioners' sugar.

B. Flour Review

Flour is the fundamental raw material of the bakeshop. Define or describe, as thoroughly as you can, each of the following products. If the product is a wheat flour, be sure to indicate whether it is a strong (high-gluten) flour or weak (low-gluten) flour.

1. Cake flour: ______________________________

____

____

2. Bread flour: ______________________________

____

____

3. Pastry flour: ______________________________

____

____

4. Rye flour: ______________________________

____

____

5. Pumpernickel: ______________________________

____

____

6. Rye meal: ______________________________

____

____

7. Patent flour: ______________________________

____

____

8. Pastry flour: ____________________

____

____

9. Whole wheat flour: ____________________

____

____

10. Bran flour: ____________________

____

____

11. Rye blend: ____________________

____

____

C. Short-Answer Questions

1. What is the weight of 1 pint of water? ____________________

2. What other liquid ingredients, commonly used in the bakeshop, weigh the same as water? ____________________

____

3. List four factors that influence the development of gluten in doughs and batters.

(a) ____________________

(b) ____________________

(c) ____________________

(d) ____________________

4. Fresh-baked goods can often become stale quickly. What are three factors that can help slow down the staling process?

(a) ____________________

(b) ____________________

(c) ____________________

5. List five functions of fats in baked goods.

(a) ______

(b) ______

(c) ______

(d) ______

(e) ______

6. List five functions of sugars in baked goods.

(a) ______

(b) ______

(c) ______

(d) ______

(e) ______

7. List eight functions of eggs in baked goods.

(a) ______

(b) ______

(c) ______

(d) ______

(e) ______

(f) ______

(g) ______

(h) ______

8. At what temperatures does yeast grow best? ______

At what temperature is yeast killed? ______

9. What are three functions of salt in baked goods?

(a) ______

(b) ______

(c) ______

D. Using Baker's Percentages

Use the percentages given to calculate the quantities needed in the following formulas. If you normally work with U.S. units of measure, fill in the blanks to the left of the percent column. If you normally work with metric units, fill in the blanks to the right of the percent column. You are provided with either the weight of flour or the total yield by weight.

I.

	U.S.	Percent	Metric
Butter	______	80%	______
Sugar	______	60%	______
Salt	______	1%	______
Ground almonds	______	50%	______
Eggs	______	16.5%	______
Pastry flour	5 lb	100%	2500 g

II.

	U.S.	Percent	Metric
Butter	______	90%	______
Sugar	______	100%	______
Sweet chocolate	______	135%	______
Egg yolks	______	100%	______
Egg whites	______	150%	______
Sugar	______	75%	______
Cake flour	______	100%	______
Yield	2 lb 5.5 oz	750%	1125 g

III.

Pastry flour	3 lb	100%	1500 g
Baking powder		5%	
Baking soda		1.25%	
Salt		1.25%	
Sugar		6.5%	
Butter		10%	
Raisins		20%	
Buttermilk		90%	

Chapter 30

Yeast Products

Bread is perhaps the most important product of the bakeshop. Procedures for making breads and other yeast products are discussed in Chapter 30. To make these products successfully, you must understand how to mix ingredients into doughs, how to control gluten development, and how to control yeast fermentation.

After studying Chapter 30, you should be able to:

1. **Prepare breads and dinner rolls.**
2. **Prepare sweet dough products.**
3. **Prepare Danish pastry and croissants.**

A. Terms

Fill in each blank with the term that is defined or described.

____________________ 1. The process by which yeast acts on carbohydrates to produce alcohol and carbon dioxide gas.

____________________ 2. The continuation of the yeast action after the dough is shaped into loaves or other products, resulting in increase in volume.

____________________ 3. A dough that is low in fat and sugar.

____________________ 4. A dough that is high in fat and sugar, and sometimes eggs.

____________________ 5. The rapid rising of a yeast dough in the oven due to production and expansion of gases.

____________________ 6. A dough in which fat is incorporated into the dough in many layers by using a folding and rolling procedure.

_______________ **7.** A yeast dough mixing method in which all ingredients are combined at once.

_______________ **8.** A dough that has fermented too long.

_______________ **9.** A dough that has not fermented long enough.

_______________ **10.** A method of deflating dough to expel carbon dioxide.

_______________ **11.** The process of shaping scaled dough into smooth, round balls.

_______________ **12.** A crescent-shaped roll made of a rolled-in dough.

_______________ **13.** Crumb topping for pastries, made of flour, butter, and sugar.

B. True/False

T F **1.** The dough arm attachment is used for mixing most yeast doughs.

T F **2.** A well-developed French bread dough should be quite sticky.

T F **3.** Club rolls and Parker House rolls are two examples of rolled-in dough products.

T F **4.** Punching is done by hitting the dough with your fist.

T F **5.** The temperature of a proof box should be set at 75°F (24°C) for most yeast products.

T F **6.** When made-up bread loaves are placed in baking pans, seams should be on the bottom.

T F **7.** Most breads and rolls are baked at a temperature of about 350°F (175°C).

T F **8.** Rich doughs are usually slightly underfermented before punching.

T F **9.** Bread in the oven is tested for doneness by testing it with a dough thermometer.

T F **10.** To maintain freshness, bread should be stored in the refrigerator.

C. Mixing Yeast Doughs

1. In the space below, write the procedure for mixing yeast doughs by the straight dough method.

2. In the space below, write the procedure for mixing rich yeast doughs by the modified straight dough method.

3. In the space below, write the procedure for mixing yeast doughs by the sponge method.

D. Using Baker's Percentages

Use the percentages given to calculate the quantities needed in the following formula. If you normally work with U.S. units of measure, fill in the blanks to the left of the percent column. If you normally work with metric units, fill in the blanks to the right of the percent column.

	U.S.	Percent	Metric
Milk	______	30%	______
Yeast	______	5%	______
Bread flour	6 oz	30%	175 g
Butter	______	40%	______
Sugar	______	20%	______
Salt	______	1.25%	______
Eggs	______	35%	______
Bread flour	14 oz	70%	425 g
Raisins	______	12.5%	______

Chapter 31

Quick Breads

This chapter deals with products that are not only very popular but also very easy to make. Consequently, this will be useful information to you in your career, so you should study it well.

After studying Chapter 31, you should be able to:

1. **Prepare baking powder biscuits and variations.**
2. **Prepare muffins, loaf breads, coffee cakes, and corn breads.**
3. **Prepare popovers.**

A. Terms

Fill in each blank with the term that is defined or described.

______________________ 1. The development of elongated holes inside muffin products.

______________________ 2. A batter that is liquid enough to be poured.

______________________ 3. A batter that is too thick to be poured, but that will drop from a spoon in lumps.

______________________ 4. A baked product made of a thin batter, leavened only by steam, and characterized by very large holes on the inside.

B. Review of Mixing Methods

1. In the space below, write the procedure for mixing doughs by the biscuit method.

2. In the space below, write the procedure for mixing batters by the muffin method.

C. Using Baker's Percentages

Use the percentages given to calculate the quantities needed in the following formula. If you normally work with U.S. units of measure, fill in the blanks to the left of the percent column. If you normally work with metric units, fill in the blanks to the right of the percent column.

	U.S.	Percent	Metric
Pastry flour	__________	100%	__________
Sugar	__________	40%	__________
Baking powder	__________	5%	__________
Baking soda	__________	0.6%	__________
Salt	__________	1.25%	__________
Walnuts	__________	25%	__________
Eggs	__________	40%	__________
Banana pulp	__________	90%	__________
Melted butter	__________	33%	__________
Yield	7 lb 8 oz	334%	3348 g

Chapter 32

Cakes and Icings

Because cakes are such delicate products, mixing and baking them requires a great deal of precision and care. It is important, then, that you study and review this chapter thoroughly in order to make superior cakes.

After studying Chapter 32, you should be able to:

1. **Demonstrate the five basic cake mixing methods.**
2. **Describe the characteristics of high-fat cakes and low-fat cakes.**
3. **Prepare high-fat, or shortened, cakes and low-fat, or foam-type, cakes.**
4. **Prepare the six basic types of icings.**
5. **Assemble and ice layer cakes, small cakes, and sheet cakes.**

A. Terms

Fill in each blank with the term that is defined or described.

______________________ **1.** A type of cake based on an egg-white foam and containing no fat.

______________________ **2.** A type of cake made with an egg-white foam and oil.

______________________ **3.** A classic cake made of equal parts butter, sugar, flour, and eggs.

______________________ **4.** A classic sponge cake made of eggs, sugar, flour, and melted butter, but with no other liquid.

______________________ **5.** An icing made by creaming together fat and sugar.

______________________ **6.** An icing made by mixing confectioners' sugar and egg whites.

_______________ 7. An icing that consists of a sugar syrup that has been crystallized to a smooth, creamy white mass.

_______________ 8. An icing that consists primarily of confectioners' sugar mixed with water.

_______________ 9. A glossy, transparent coating that gives a shine to baked products.

B. Review of Cake Mixing Methods

1. In the space below, explain how to mix cakes by the creaming method. Be sure to include all the necessary steps, and number the steps.

2. In the space below, explain how to mix cakes by the two-stage method. Be sure to include all the necessary steps, and number the steps.

3. In the space below, explain how to mix angel food cakes. Be sure to include all the necessary steps, and number the steps.

4. In the space below, explain how to mix genoise-type sponge cakes. Include all the necessary steps, and number the steps.

5. In the space below, explain how to mix chiffon cakes. Write the procedure in the form of numbered steps.

C. Review of Icing Preparations

1. Fondant must be warmed for use, but it should not be heated above 100°F (38°C). Why? ____________

____

2. How do you make chocolate fondant? ____________

____

3. Name and describe the three main types of buttercream.

   (a) ____________

   ____

   (b) ____________

   ____

   (c) ____________

   ____

4. What is decorator's buttercream? ____________

____

____

5. What is royal icing used for? ____________

6. Briefly describe how to make and how to store royal icing.

____

____

____

____

7. Briefly describe two methods for icing cupcakes.

   (a) ____________

   ____

   (b) ____________

   ____

8. Flat icings are handled and applied in the same way as what other type of icing? ______________________

____

9. What is a foam icing? ____

____

D. Using Baker's Percentages

Use the percentages given to calculate the quantities needed in the following formula. If you normally work with U.S. units of measure, fill in the blanks to the left of the percent column. If you normally work with metric units, fill in the blanks to the right of the percent column.

	U.S.	Percent	Metric
Flour	________	100%	________
Salt	________	2%	________
Baking powder	________	2%	________
Emulsified shortening	________	67%	________
Sugar	________	117%	________
Nonfat milk solids	________	6%	________
Water	________	45%	________
Eggs	________	67%	________
Raisins	________	25%	________
Yield	8 lb 8 oz	430%	3865 g

Chapter 33

Cookies

Like most kitchen and bakeshop tasks, learning to make cookies easily and efficiently is primarily a matter of developing manual skills. But like most food service tasks, it also requires some understanding of theory and basic principles. This chapter will help you review those principles.

After studying Chapter 33, you should be able to:

1. **List the factors responsible for crispness, softness, chewiness, and spread in cookies.**
2. **Demonstrate the three basic cookie mixing methods.**
3. **Prepare the seven basic cookies types: dropped, bagged, rolled, molded, icebox, bar, and sheet.**
4. **Prepare pans for, bake, and cool cookies.**

A. Terms

Fill in each blank with the term that is defined or described.

______________________ **1.** Readily absorbing moisture.

______________________ **2.** A cookie made of coconut mixed with meringue.

______________________ **3.** A rich, rather crumbly Scottish cookie made of butter, flour, and sugar; some variations also contain egg.

______________________ **4.** Finger-shaped soft cookies made from a sponge batter.

The following terms refer to categories of cookies based on makeup method.

_______________ **5.** Cookies cut from refrigerated, sausage-shaped pieces of dough.

_______________ **6.** Cookies pressed from a pastry bag.

_______________ **7.** Cookies made with a cookie cutter.

_______________ **8.** Cookies made by spreading dough or batter in sheet pans, baking, and then cutting out squares or rectangles.

_______________ **9.** Cookies made from lumps of dough dropped onto baking pans.

_______________ **10.** Cookies made from cylinders of dough flattened onto sheet pans, baked, then cut crosswise into pieces.

_______________ **11.** Cookies made from equal pieces of dough cut from a cylinder, placed on sheet pans, then pressed flat.

B. Review of Cookie Mixing Methods

1. Using numbered steps, describe the creaming method for mixing cookies.

2. Using numbered steps, describe the one-stage method for mixing cookies.

C. Short-Answer Questions

1. A cookie dough is more likely to spread when baked if its content of granulated sugar is ____________________.

2. The main reason for shaping cookies uniformly during makeup is ____________________.

3. Cookie dough to be rolled out with a rolling pin should be at what temperature? ____________________

4. What is likely to happen to cookies baked at too high a temperature? ____________________

5. What should be done with freshly baked cookies before they are put in containers for storage? ____________________

____

6. How much flour should be used for dusting when rolling out cookie dough with a rolling pin? ____________________

____

7. What is the main indication of doneness when cookies are baked? ____________________

8. If a rich cookie dough burns too easily when baked, what can be done to prevent burning? ____________________

____

D. Using Baker's Percentages

Use the percentages given to calculate the quantities needed in the following formula. If you normally work with U.S. units of measure, fill in the blanks to the left of the percent column. If you normally work with metric units, fill in the blanks to the right of the percent column.

	U.S.	Percent	Metric
Butter	______	67%	______
Brown sugar	______	133%	______
Salt	______	1.5%	______
Eggs	______	33%	______
Vanilla	______	3%	______
Milk	______	8%	______
Pastry flour	1 lb 14 oz	100%	900 g
Baking powder	______	4%	______
Baking soda	______	2%	______
Rolled oats	______	83%	______
Raisins	______	50%	______

Chapter 34

Pies and Pastries

Many kinds of products are presented in Chapter 34, and the techniques used to prepare them are important ones. The various review exercises here will help you study the various procedures involved in pastry making.

After studying Chapter 34, you should be able to:

1. **Prepare flaky pie dough and mealy pie dough.**
2. **Prepare crumb crusts and short, or cookie, crusts.**
3. **Assemble and bake pies.**
4. **Prepare the following pie fillings: fruit fillings using the cooked juice method, the cooked fruit method, and the old-fashioned method; custard or soft fillings; cream pie fillings; and chiffon fillings.**
5. **Prepare puff pastry dough and puff dough products.**
6. **Prepare éclair paste and éclair paste products.**
7. **Prepare standard meringues and meringue desserts.**
8. **Prepare fruit desserts.**

A. Terms

Fill in each blank with the term that is defined or described.

____________________ **1.** A type of dough that is mixed like pie dough but rolled and folded like puff paste.

____________________ **2.** A dessert consisting of ice cream covered with meringue and browned in the oven.

____________________ **3.** Starch that thickens liquids without cooking, because it has been precooked.

_______________ 4. A dessert made of layers of puff pastry alternating with layers of pastry cream or other cream.

_______________ 5. French name for eclair paste.

_______________ 6. A type of meringue made with boiling syrup.

_______________ 7. Tiny cream puffs, often filled with ice cream and served with chocolate syrup.

_______________ 8. A type of meringue made with a warmed mixture of egg whites and sugar.

_______________ 9. A type of pie filling that is lightened by the addition of whipped egg whites.

_______________ 10. A starch that makes a clear gel when cooked and that does not break down when frozen.

_______________ 11. A crisp disk of baked meringue containing nuts.

_______________ 12. A baked dessert made of sliced, sugared apples topped with a crumb or streussel topping flavored with cinnamon.

_______________ 13. A baked meringue shell filled with ice cream.

_______________ 14. Baking a pie or tart shell without a filling.

B. Pie Review

1. The main types of pie dough are _______________ and _______________.

2. The difference between the two main types of pie dough mostly depends on _______________

   _______________.

3. Water for pie dough should be at what temperature? ________

4. What are two functions of salt in pie dough? _______________

   ____

   ____

5. If shortening is used to make pie dough, what type of shortening is the correct one to use? _______________

   ____

6. The two basic steps in the rubbed dough method are _______________

   ____

7. A basic graham cracker crust is made with what ingredients?

   ____

8. Assume you have made a fruit pie filling by the cooked juice method. At about what temperature should the filling be when the pie shell is filled? ________________________________

9. Vanilla cream pie filling is thickened with ________________ .

10. The best thickening agent to use for fruit pie fillings is ________________ .

11. To prevent lumping, starch must be mixed with ________________ or with ________________ before being added to a hot liquid.

12. In the space below, list the four ingredients in basic pie dough, then write the procedure for mixing the ingredients to make a dough. Use numbered steps. Be sure to explain the difference between the two main types of dough.

Ingredients: ________________

____

____

____

Procedure:

13. In the space below, explain how to make fruit pie fillings using the cooked juice method. Write the procedure in the form of numbered steps.

14. In the space below, explain how to make fruit pie fillings using the cooked fruit method. Write the procedure in the form of numbered steps.

C. True/False

T F 1. Eclair paste is made with pastry flour.

T F 2. Puff paste is rolled and folded with the same number of folds as Danish pastry.

T F 3. Puff pastry is leavened with baking powder.

T F 4. Eclair paste is leavened with baking soda.

T F 5. Puff paste is refrigerated briefly between turns, especially if the bakeshop is warm.

T F 6. Butter to be rolled into puff paste must be well chilled and hard so that it won't ooze out of the dough.

T F 7. A 4-fold gets its name because it results in four times as many layers in the dough each time it is done.

T F 8. Eclairs are baked at a low temperature to give them time to puff up.

T F 9. The flour mixture for eclair paste is chilled before the eggs are added.

T F 10. Hard meringues are baked at a low temperature so that they will dry out but will not brown.

T F 11. Meringue pie topping is made with about 4 oz of sugar per pound of egg whites (250 g sugar per kilogram of egg whites).

D. Using Baker's Percentages

Use the percentages given to calculate the quantities needed in the following formulas. If you normally work with U.S. units of measure, fill in the blanks to the left of the percent column. If you normally work with metric units, fill in the blanks to the right of the percent column. You are provided with either the weight of flour or the total yield by weight.

	U.S.	Percent	Metric
I.			
Pastry flour	________	100%	________
Shortening	________	70%	________
Salt	________	2%	________
Water	________	30%	________
Yield	14 lb	202%	6000 g

II.

Pastry flour	4 lb	100%	2000 g
Sugar	______	17%	______
Butter	______	50%	______
Egg yolks	______	8%	______
Water	______	25%	______
Salt	______	1%	______

Chapter 35

Creams, Custards, Puddings, Frozen Desserts, and Sauces

Like the previous chapter, this chapter presents a wide variety of techniques and products. Some of these products, like pastry cream, are used as components of many different kinds of desserts and pastries, so it is important to know them well. Since many of the recipes are based on egg custards, it will also help you to review what you learned about eggs in Chapter 24.

After studying Chapter 35, you should be able to:

1. **Cook sugar syrups to the seven stages of hardness.**
2. **Prepare crème anglaise, pastry cream, and baked custard.**
3. **Prepare starch-thickened puddings and baked puddings.**
4. **Prepare bavarians, chiffons, mousses, and dessert soufflés.**
5. **Assemble frozen desserts.**
6. **Prepare dessert sauces.**

A. Terms

Fill in each blank with the term that is defined or described.

_______________ 1. A custard sauce made of sweetened, vanilla-flavored milk thickened with egg yolks.

_______________ 2. A flavored simple syrup, used to moisten and flavor some cakes.

_______________ 3. A thick stirred custard thickened with starch as well as with eggs; used as a pastry and pie filling and as a pudding.

______________________________ 4. A baked custard made in a caramel-lined mold, so that it has a caramel topping when turned out of the mold.

______________________________ 5. A white cornstarch pudding, often flavored with almond extract.

______________________________ 6. A pudding similar to a cornstarch pudding but also containing eggs.

______________________________ 7. A dessert consisting of alternating layers of ice cream and fruit or syrup in a tall, narrow glass.

______________________________ 8. Ice cream containing no eggs.

______________________________ 9. The increase in volume of ice cream during freezing due to incorporation of air.

______________________________ 10. A chilled dessert made of flavored custard sauce, gelatin, and whipped cream.

______________________________ 11. A soft or creamy dessert made light or fluffy by the addition of whipped cream or whipped egg whites or both.

______________________________ 12. A dessert consisting of one or two scoops of ice cream or sherbet in a dish or glass, topped with any of a number of syrups, fruits, or toppings.

______________________________ 13. A molded ice cream dessert consisting of two or more layers of different ice creams.

______________________________ 14. A baked, pudding-like dessert lightened with whipped egg whites.

______________________________ 15. A frozen dessert similar to ice cream but with a lower butterfat content.

______________________________ 16. A dessert consisting of a pear half, chocolate sauce, and toasted almonds on top of vanilla ice cream.

______________________________ 17. A frozen dessert made of fruit juices, water, sugar, and sometimes egg whites, but containing no milk products.

______________________________ 18. A frozen dessert similar to the one described in number 17 but with a coarse, crystalline texture and made without egg whites.

______________________________ 19. A dessert or pie filling containing gelatin and whipped egg whites.

______________________________ 20. A dessert consisting of a peach half and raspberry sauce on top of vanilla ice cream.

______________________________ 21. The browning of sugar caused by heat.

B. Review of Sugar Cooking

1. A simple syrup is a solution of equal parts ____________ and ____________.

2. Dessert syrup is a simple syrup plus ____________.

3. When a syrup is boiled, moisture gradually evaporates, and the temperature of the syrup gradually ____________.

4. If a syrup is cooked to 300°F (150°C) and then cooled, its texture will be ____________.

5. If a syrup is cooked until it turns light brown, the resulting product is called ____________.

6. If an acid, such as ____________, is added to a syrup before cooking, some of the sugar turns to ____________. The advantage of this is ____________ ____________.

7. When you want to cook a syrup to a certain stage of doneness, the tool you need to accurately test for doneness is ____________.

8. When the instructions in a candy recipe say to "wash down the sides of the pan with a brush dipped in water," the purpose of this direction is ____________ ____________.

C. Review of Basic Custards and Creams

1. The basic ingredients of crème anglaise are ____________, ____________, ____________, and vanilla.

2. Crème anglaise is completely cooked when it reaches a temperature of ____________.

3. Why is a double boiler generally used to make crème anglaise? ____________ ____________

4. Why is it important to use clean, sanitary equipment when making crème anglaise and pastry cream?

____

____

5. Why is it important to chill pastry cream quickly after it is cooked? ____

____

6. After pastry cream is cooked, it is poured into ______________ pans so that it will cool quickly.

7. What is the advantage of baking custards in a hot-water bath? ____

____

8. When making baked custards, what is the advantage of scalding the milk before adding it to the eggs?

____

____

9. In the space below, write the procedure for preparing crème anglaise. Use numbered steps.

10. In the space that follows, write the procedure for preparing vanilla pastry cream.

D. True/False

T F 1. Lemon pie filling is made using the same technique as vanilla pastry cream.

T F 2. A boiling syrup that is at the crack stage is hotter than a boiling syrup at the hard ball stage.

T F 3. Corn syrup should not be added to a boiling sugar syrup because it may cause crystallization.

T F 4. French-style ice cream contains egg yolks.

T F 5. For sanitary reasons, crème anglaise should be brought to a boil to kill bacteria.

T F 6. When scalded milk is added to egg yolks, it should be added all at once.

T F 7. A dessert soufflé is always baked at a low temperature (about 300°F/150°C) to give the soufflé time to rise properly.

T F 8. If both whipped cream and whipped egg whites must be added to a chocolate mousse, the whipped cream is always added first.

T F 9. If egg whites for a dessert soufflé are beaten with some sugar, this helps to make the soufflé more stable.

T F 10. Butterscotch pudding is made by making vanilla pudding with extra butter, and adding scotch flavoring.

T F 11. Frozen mousses can be still-frozen (not churn-frozen in an ice cream freezer) because they contain whipped cream or whipped egg whites.

T F 12. A coupe is basically the same as a sundae.

E. Portion Cost

Cost out the following recipe. For prices of the ingredients, use figures supplied by your instructor or the *Sample Prices* in the Appendix of this *Study Guide*.

ITEM: **CHOCOLATE CREAM PIE**

Ingredient	Recipe Quantity	AP Quantity	Price	Total Amount
Flour	12 oz	______	______	______
Shortening	8 oz	______	______	______
Water	4 oz	______	______	______
Milk	2 qt	______	______	______
Sugar	1 lb	______	______	______
Eggs	8	______	______	______
Cornstarch	5 oz	______	______	______
Sweet chocolate	4 oz	______	______	______
Bitter chocolate	4 oz	______	______	______
Butter	4 oz	______	______	______
Vanilla	1 oz	______	______	______
			Total cost	______
			Number of portions	24
			Cost per portion	______

Portion Cost—Metric

Cost out the following recipe. For prices of the ingredients, use figures supplied by your instructor or the *Sample Prices* in the Appendix of this *Study Guide*.

ITEM: **CHOCOLATE CREAM PIE**

Ingredient	Recipe Quantity	AP Quantity	Price	Total Amount
Flour	375 g	______	______	______
Shortening	250 g	______	______	______
Water	125 g	______	______	______
Milk	2 L	______	______	______
Sugar	500 g	______	______	______
Eggs	8	______	______	______
Cornstarch	150 g	______	______	______
Sweet chocolate	125 g	______	______	______
Bitter chocolate	125 g	______	______	______
Butter	125 g	______	______	______
Vanilla	30 mL	______	______	______
			Total cost	______
			Number of portions	24
			Cost per portion	______

Appendix: Sample Prices

Your instructors may want you to use the prices on current invoices when you do the Portion Cost exercises in this manual. If not, you may use the following hypothetical prices. Do not worry about whether or not these prices seem realistic. Prices change, but you can still practice the calculations with these numbers.

Meat, Poultry, and Fish

Beef brisket	\$ 1.80 per lb	\$ 3.89 per kg
Beef, ground	1.39 per lb	3.19 per kg
Chicken parts	0.85 per lb	1.85 per kg
Italian pork sausages	1.49 per lb	3.29 per kg
Sole fillets	5.99 per lb	13.00 per kg

Produce and Frozen Vegetables

Artichokes	\$ 0.45 each	\$ 0.45 each
Cabbage	0.25 per lb	0.55 per kg
Carrots	0.30 per lb	0.65 per kg
Leeks	1.10 per lb	2.40 per kg
Lemons	0.20 each	0.20 each
Lettuce, iceberg	0.80 per head	0.80 per head
Mushrooms	1.25 per lb	2.75 per kg
Onions, yellow	0.30 per lb	0.65 per kg
Peas, frozen	2.20 per 2½ lb pack	1.95 per kg
Peppers, green bell	0.50 per lb	1.15 per kg
Peppers, red bell	2.49 per lb	5.49 per kg
Peppers, Italian	0.80 per lb	1.75 per kg
Potatoes, all-purpose	0.20 per lb	0.45 per kg
Potatoes, baking, "100's" (8-oz average weight)	0.30 per lb	0.65 per kg
Shallots	1.50 per lb	3.50 per kg
Squash, butternut	0.35 per lb	0.75 per kg
Tomatoes	0.50 per lb	1.20 per kg

Dairy and Eggs

Butter	$ 1.70 per lb	$ 3.75 per kg
Milk	0.45 per qt	0.45 per L
Heavy cream	2.69 per qt	2.69 per L
Sour cream	1.09 per lb	2.40 per kg
Cheese, Gruyère	4.00 per lb	8.50 per kg
Cheese, Parmesan	6.00 per lb	13.00 per kg
Eggs, large	0.89 per dozen	0.89 per dozen

Groceries

Beets, canned	$ 0.60 per #2½ can	$ 0.60 per #2½ can
Breadcrumbs, dry	0.79 per lb	1.79 per kg
Bulgur wheat	0.79 per lb	1.79 per kg
Chili powder	0.75 per oz	2.70 per 100 g
Chocolate, bitter	3.98 per lb	8.79 per kg
Chocolate, sweet	3.69 per lb	8.19 per kg
Cornstarch	0.59 per lb	1.29 per kg
Flour	0.15 per lb	0.35 per kg
Ginger, ground	1.40 per oz	5.00 per 100 g
Mayonnaise	6.50 per gal	1.65 per L
Oil, olive	3.29 per qt	3.29 per L
Oil, salad/vegetable	4.60 per gal	1.20 per L
Pepper, black	0.45 per oz	1.59 per 100 g
Raisins	1.09 per lb	2.39 per kg
Salt	0.15 per lb	0.35 per kg
Shortening	0.55 per lb	1.20 per kg
Soy sauce	1.25 per pt	2.50 per L
Spaghetti	0.79 per lb	1.75 per kg
Sugar, brown	0.45 per lb	1.00 per kg
Sugar, granulated	0.30 per lb	0.65 per kg
Tomato paste	0.70 per 1-lb can	0.75 per 500-g can
Tomato purée	0.45 per 1-lb can	0.50 per 500-g can
Tomatoes, whole, canned	0.35 per lb	0.75 per kg
Tomatoes, #10 can	2.10 per can	2.10 per can
Vanilla	10.00 per qt	10.00 per L
Vinegar, red wine	0.75 per qt	0.75 per L

Miscellaneous

Beef stock	$ 0.30 per qt	$ 0.30 per L
Chicken stock	0.25 per qt	0.25 per L
Fish stock	0.50 per qt	0.50 per L
Sherry wine	7.00 per qt	7.00 per L

fotofolio

by Eugene W. Metcalf and Frank Maresca. Photographs by Charles Bechtold

INTRODUCTION

Toy ray guns conjure a wealth of meanings and associations. Their outlandish shapes and fanciful colors evoke fond childhood memories of Buck Rogers and Captain Video, of backyard spaceships that blasted off for high adventure in the endless reaches of space. The stuff of fancy, toy ray guns are powered by pure imagination, by our almost unlimited capacity to wonder. Yet they represent other things as well. They are weapons intended to protect us from our deepest fears of the dark unknown, and they remind us of our vulnerability in the face of an endless and mysterious cosmos. Ray guns are testimony to the fact that we often imagine even the majesty of space as a backdrop for our conflicts and struggles, and that humankind finally set foot on the moon only as the result of a competitive, war-like "race" between two superpower nations. From the exuberant Art Deco disintegrator pistols of the 1930s, to the streamlined tin-litho sparkers of the 1950s and the darkly post-apocalyptic nitro-blasters of today, toy ray guns express and represent our dreams, fears, and fantasies.

BUCK ROGERS AND THE POPULAR DISCOVERY OF SPACE

The first toy ray guns were produced in the 1930s. Part of the Buck Rogers craze that swept the United States, they were an important by-product of, and influence on the popularizing of space that occurred in the early decades of the twentieth century. Our entry into the domain of space began during the 1920s and 1930s when an American scientist, Robert H. Goddard, began the first early tests of liquid fueled rockets. Disproving the theory that rockets could not move forward in space because there was no air to push against, Goddard discovered the basic principles of rocket science. Yet, ironically, it was not Goddard, the father of space travel, who first caught the public's attention and popularized space exploration. It was a far more fanciful and romantic character, Buck Rogers.

Anthony "Buck" Rogers was born in August of 1928 in an early edition of the pulp magazine, *Amazing Stories*. Introduced in the story "Armageddon 2419" by Philip Nowlan, Rogers was an air force officer who lapsed into a coma and awakened in the 25th century where he found America in ruins and the world dominated by Mongolians from inland China. Quickly discovering the marvels of this future world, including anti-gravity belts, rocket pistols, and space ships, Rogers and his cohorts, the lovely Wilma Deering and the intrepid scientist Dr. Huer, set out to free the world and battle evil and injustice.

At about this same moment the editors of the National Newspaper Syndicate began looking for a new adventure comic strip, and Philip Nowlan and illustrator Dick Calkins were commissioned to inaugurate a syndicated comic based on Nowlan's story. Anthony Rogers' name was changed to "Buck" to recall the popular heroes of America's Wild West and the new Buck Rogers comic strip made its first appearance in January of 1929. An almost instant success, it ran for over forty years. A radio adaptation was broadcast from 1932 to 1947, movies were made, and television versions of Buck's adventures appeared in both the 1950s and 1980s. Buck Rogers became *the* American space hero and one of the greatest pop culture heroes of all time. So insatiable was the public appetite for the daring space traveler that he spawned another popular space hero, Flash Gordon, who was created in 1934 by King Features to compete with the Buck Rogers comic strip. Like Buck, Flash soon became a comic book hero and radio star and, over the years, he appeared in movies and on television. By the end of the 1930s, Buck Rogers and Flash Gordon had transformed space into a popular and well-known adventure setting. More importantly, until the actual inauguration of the space race in the 1950s and early 1960s, these two fictional characters were probably responsible for teaching most people what they knew about outer space.

The introduction of the first metal toy ray guns by Daisy Manufacturing Co. was carefully planned to coincide with the developing popularity of Buck Rogers and became one of the most successful marketing campaigns in the history of the American toy industry. Daisy designers first convinced Nowlan and Calkins to redesign the hand guns, helmets, and holsters portrayed in Buck's adventures so that they could be exactly duplicated by Daisy. In February of 1934, after the Buck Rogers comic strip and radio show had developed a significant following and a strong market potential for Buck Rogers toys, Daisy introduced their first Buck Rogers gun, the XZ-31 Rocket Pistol. Before the introduction of the XZ-31, Daisy had already convinced the J.L. Hudson department store in Detroit to make "Buck Rogers in the 25th Century" their Christmas theme, and to install a large rocket ship and set of Martian figures in their toy department. Daisy then used these same props when it finally introduced its Buck Rogers gun at the prestigious American Toy Fair.

Despite initial skepticism about the XZ-31 (many toy buyers at the toy fair thought Buck Rogers was a cowboy!), Macy's Department Store in New York City agreed to promote the gun in exchange for a one week exclusive on its sales. Using the rocket ship and extra-terrestrial figures from J.L. Hudson, Macy's promotion was so successful that, on the day the guns went on sale, over 2,000 people stood in line outside their doors to buy the Rocket Pistol. As the week went on the crowds grew, and in order to keep Macy's supplied, Daisy kept trucks on the road every day from their Michigan plant.

Following this first week promotion, the XZ-31 was shipped to stores across the country, including Gimbel's, Macy's rival department store in New York City. As soon as Gimbel's received their guns, they cut the price below the forty-nine cents which Macy's had been charging. This started a price war between the two stores. Within a few weeks Gimbel's was pricing their guns at two for nineteen cents—substantially below their cost! Prices of the Rocket Pistol changed almost hourly in each of the stores, except when one of them ran out of toys, at which time the other store raised its price. While this was going on, Daisy exacerbated and profited from this situation by sending people into whichever store had the lowest price and buying back its guns which were then sold to the other store. According to Cass Hough, Daisy sales manager at the time, "during those first two weeks the Gimbel's and Macy's toy departments looked like a cyclone had struck, and people were still lining up to buy (Lesser, 168–227)."

Soon almost every toy store in the country was clamoring for shipments of the XZ-31 and Daisy could not get enough steel material or cardboard boxes to keep up with the production demand. For Christmas that year, Daisy developed a Buck Rogers holster and helmet to go with the Rocket Pistol, and the next year they produced a new Buck Rogers gun, the XZ-38 Disintegrator Pistol, as well as a smaller version of the Rocket Pistol, the XZ-35. In 1936 Daisy brought out one of the most colorful Buck Rogers toy guns, the XZ-44 Liquid Helium Water Pistol, finished in bright yellow and red lightning bolts. (It also came in a plainer, but no less striking, copper color.) After World War II, Daisy used the existing tools and dies from the Disintegrator Pistol to create their last Buck Rogers gun. Called the U-235 Atomic Pistol, this gun reflected the then current fascination with atomic energy. Before and after the war, Daisy was not the only company to produce toy ray guns, and other manufacturers flooded the market with Buck Rogers items. No other character, except Mickey Mouse, has ever been associated with more products.

RAY GUNS, CHILDHOOD, AND THE ESCAPE TO SPACE

The phenomenal popularity of the Buck Rogers ray guns was due to more than effective marketing and promotion. Crucial to the success of these toys was a new view of childhood which, together with the developing popular conception of space, joined to make ray guns an important tool in the acting out of modern ideas of fantasy and escape.

By the early years of the twentieth century, American ideas of childhood had experienced a significant change. No longer viewed as small adults, whose primary value was their ability to help support the family economic system, children were treasured instead for their emotional contributions, for the warmth and affection they evoked. In this new romantic view, children were valued for their non-adult qualities, for their representation to adults of an escape from the pressures and concerns of the adult world. Thought to be a unique world set apart from the dull, workaday realm of their parents, the world of children came to be epitomized by J.M. Barrie's beloved children's book, *Peter Pan*. Thus the world of children was understood as a timeless, make-believe fantasy land where boys and girls were unrestrained by the codes which bound their parents and could experience true fun and unending play. Toys became the necessary tools of this playful world of children, and were viewed as an important part of a happy and successful childhood (Cross, 81–120).

The popular view of space first presented by Buck Rogers fit perfectly into this new conception of childhood. Understood as another territory of Never-Never Land, the far reaches of the universe came to be imagined as a magical world where children and adults alike could escape the mundane and everyday. Whether zooming through space in rocket ships, floating above the earth in anti-gravity belts, or zapping green aliens with disintegrator guns, the fantasies of space represented an alternative to life's often harsher realities, especially during the dark days of the Depression.

The fantastic nature of space adventure is wonderfully expressed in the highly imaginative shapes and forms of the toy ray guns that exemplify this alternative world. Included among the countless ray guns produced since the 1930s are sleek silver cap guns with ruby sparking chambers, copper "disintegrator pistols" bristling with flamboyant fins and flashy fluted barrels, and plastic bubble shooters in cartoon colors and outrageous comic book shapes. Abstract aluminum "spinrays" sprout flower-like propellers, splashy yellow blasters are emblazoned with hot lightning-bolt designs, and Japanese tin pistols reveal tiny scenes of starry skies, exploding rockets, and lunar landscapes upon their intricately drawn surfaces. Unconventional in function as well as form, these unlikely armaments shoot smoke rings and colored lights, spurt water, discharge paper streamers, and disarm their targets with soap bubbles and bursts of baking soda.

Such whimsical creations are harmless in nature and innocent in intent. But toy ray guns also evoke darker associations that make them paradoxical as objects of play. Conceived to accompany explorers on their journey into dark unknown regions of the cosmos, they call to mind the aggressive and even hostile actions that have too often characterized our encounters with new frontiers. In fact, the narratives of space adventure mimic the mythic tales of the "discovery" and "settlement" of America's Wild West. Like Buck Rogers, space adventurers have often been modeled on the heroic image of the American cowboy. Similarly, ray guns recall the legendary pearl-handled six-shooter. Like their counterpart in nineteenth century America, these imaginary firearms of the future not only serve to protect or keep the peace, but also evidence our tendency to confront new worlds and alien peoples with distrust and the threat of conquest and aggression.

RAY GUNS AND POST WAR CULTURE

The Second World War changed the popular experience of space technology from an innocent fantasy to the potential of a real-life terror. After German V-2 rockets decimated London and American bombs fell on Japan, the idea of jet propulsion, atomic energy, and space travel could never again be purely benign or fanciful. Perhaps it was, in part, this unease with the dawning space age that contributed to the frequent, disturbing sightings of unidentified flying objects, or UFOs, which began in the United States in the late 1940s.

The advent of television in the 1950s also increased the popular interest in space travel and exploration. Like the Buck Rogers radio dramas of the 1930s, the television "space operas" of the 1950s broadcast tales of space adventures to a wide audience. Television added a dramatic visual dimension to the voices and sound effects of radio, encouraging children to participate even more actively in the fantasies unfolding upon the screen. Space toys became necessary props in these playful reenactments. As in the decades before the war, advertisers were quick to associate their products with the heroes and activities of children's space programs, offering toy premiums like the Space Cadet Membership Kit from Kellogg's Cereal, Captain Video's Electronic Video Goggles from Powerhouse Candy, the set of flying saucer rings from Post Toasties, and the interplanetary coin album from Schwinn Bicycles.

The first TV space series was "Captain Video," which aired in June of 1949. In the 1950s, the small screen was virtually invaded by space heroes like "Rocky Jones, Space Ranger," "Rod Brown of the Rocket Rangers," and "Commando Cody, Sky Marshall of the Universe." Perhaps the most popular space program was "Tom Corbett, Space Cadet." Premiering in 1950, it remained on the air three times a week for five years and appeared on all four commercial TV networks. Tom Corbett was the most heavily merchandised television space show with over 135 products bearing the Space Cadet's famous name. Four toy ray guns identified with Tom Corbett were sold by the Louis Marx Co.: a tin-litho clicker, a flashlight pistol, and two space rifles. Among the other television space shows used to promote ray guns as props for fantastic children's play was "Space Patrol." First broadcast nationally in June of 1951, this program was the inspiration for five space guns, including two smoke ring guns, a flashlight pistol, a rocket dart gun, and the rare Space Patrol Autosonic Rifle.

Fueled by the popularity of television space shows, comic strips, and films like "Forbidden Planet," space toys and ray guns became a toy shop staple in the 1950s and 1960s. Although partially eclipsed by Davy Crockett and the cowboy craze of the mid 1950s, the production and sales of space toys picked up again in 1957 when the launching of the Soviet Union's Sputnik satellite once again refocused the attention of Americans on outer space. After this date, many space toys were advertised to be more "realistic." Modeled on actual space vehicles like satellite launchers and ballistic missiles, they were said to be "scaled from official blueprints." Ray guns, however, continued to be pure invention. Never copied from real firearms or a part of the real space program, toy guns like the Martian Guided Whistle "Bloon" Gun and the Strato Gun (advertised as "earth's only interplanetary cap pistol") continued to reflect the themes of fantasy and escapist adventure that had first inspired the production of space guns in the 1930s.

While perpetuating the escapist fantasy of their predecessors, toy ray guns from the postwar decades were also differentiated by a few important factors. Unlike the earlier guns which were created largely from heavy stamped or die-cast metal, the later ones were more likely to be fabricated of plastic in the United States. Injection molding machines, which force liquid plastic into standardized molds, had appeared as early as the 1930s, but it was not until the 1950s that improvements in plastics technology had begun to revolutionize the American toy industry. Although extraordinary die-cast productions like the ornate Hubley Atomic Disintegrator were still being produced, American ray gun production excelled in the use of plastics technology. In fact, the art of plastic toy making reached new heights with such creations as the powerfully sculpted Smoke Ring Gun by Nu-Age Products, the outlandish Automatic Repeating Bubble Shooting Gun by Arliss, and the beautiful and delicately proportioned Planet Jet by Renwal Manufacturing.

Another element that distinguished postwar ray guns was their more widespread production and distribution. Although before World War II all toy ray guns had been made in the United States for a largely American market, in the decades following the war, many of these toys were produced in Japan for a market that was increasingly international. Tin toys were a specialty of the Japanese. In the late 1950s, as a part of the postwar Japanese economic recovery, Japanese manufacturers began to export significant numbers of lithographed tin ray guns, rockets, and other space toys into the United States and other parts of the world. While thinner and less durable than their American tin counterparts, the Japanese ray guns possessed fanciful surface designs and strikingly beautiful color combinations which were generally more sophisticated and interesting than those on the American guns. With their highly visual and imaginative graphics, Japanese tin guns, like the diminutive Space Control Gun by TN and the whimsical Super Sonic Gun by Daiya, are brilliant examples of the art of tin toy making.

But it was not only the Americans and Japanese who made ray guns. In the two decades following World War II, these toys were produced in numerous other countries. Among some of the most interesting guns from this period are those fabricated in England where, like those made in the United States, such toys were often associated with comic and television space heroes such as Dr. Who and Ace Hart. The most notable of these characters was Dan Dare, the central protagonist in a feature which ran for many years in the boys magazine *Eagle*. A "fearless pilot of the future," Dare did not drink or swear. He fired only in self-defense and always told the truth. Many toy ray guns were produced using Dare's name, including the Dan Dare Cosmic Ray Gun by Palitoy, a striking plastic flashlight gun with dramatically backswept handle and sights.

The late 1950s and 1960s represent the apex of Japanese and European ray gun manufacture as well as the end of the great age of American toy space guns. By the late 1960s and 1970s, high-tech electronic ray guns were being introduced and the fabrication of the majority of toy space guns began moving to Hong Kong, Taiwan, and China. With these developments, a new, and as yet unexplored chapter in the history of toy ray guns began and the "classic" period of toy ray guns came to an end.

Eugene W. Metcalf, Jr.
March 1999
Oxford, Ohio

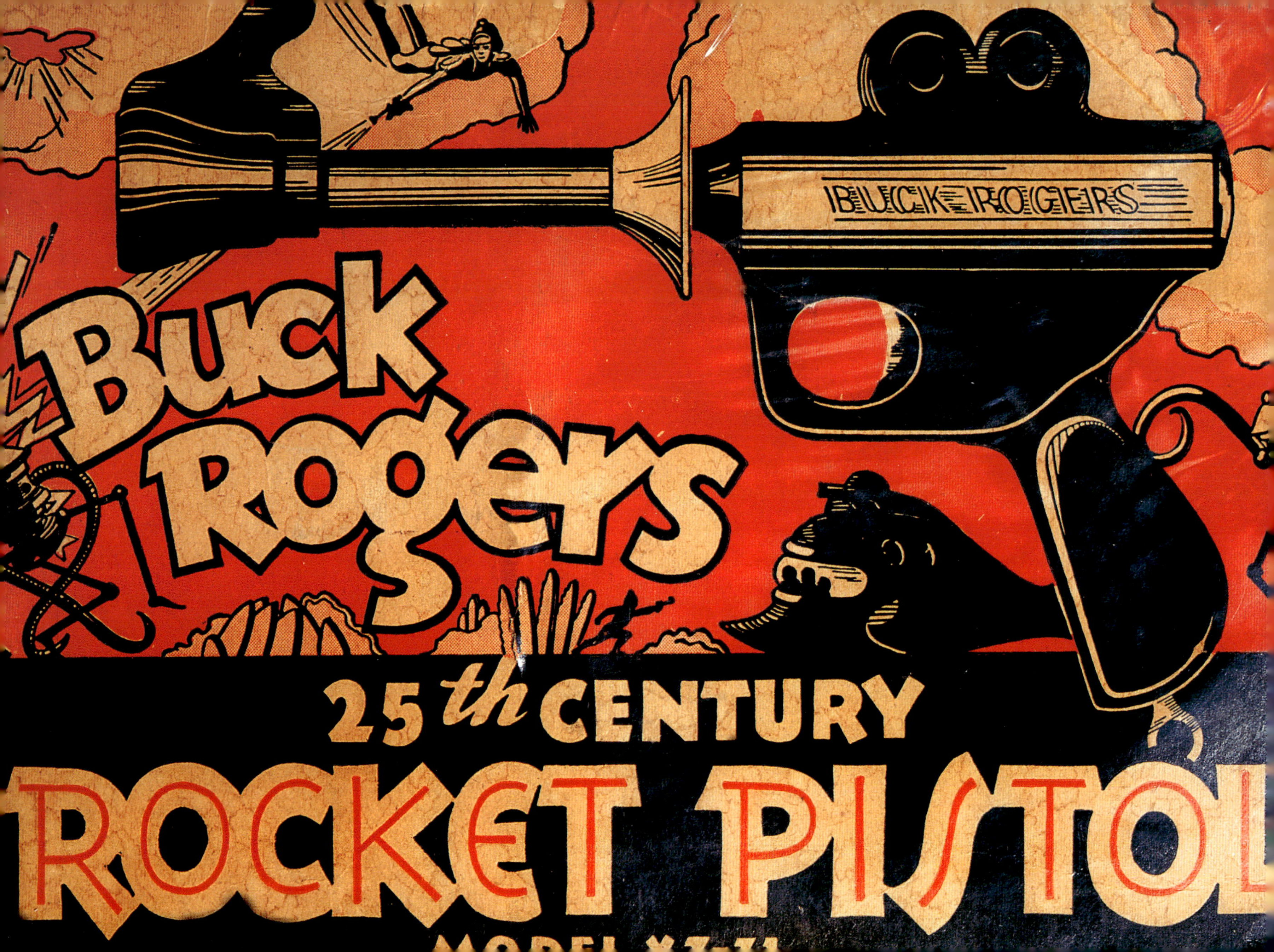
BUCK ROGERS
Buck Rogers
25th CENTURY
ROCKET PISTOL

Buck Rogers Rocket Pistol, XZ-35, pressed steel, 5½ x 7 in., Daisy Manufacturing Co., U.S.A. 1935

Buck Rogers Disintegrator Pistol, XZ-38, pressed steel with copper finish, 6 x 10 in., Daisy Manufacturing Co., U.S.A. 1936

Nu-Matic Paper Popper, pressed steel, 6 x 6½ in., Langson Manufacturing Co., U.S.A. 1936

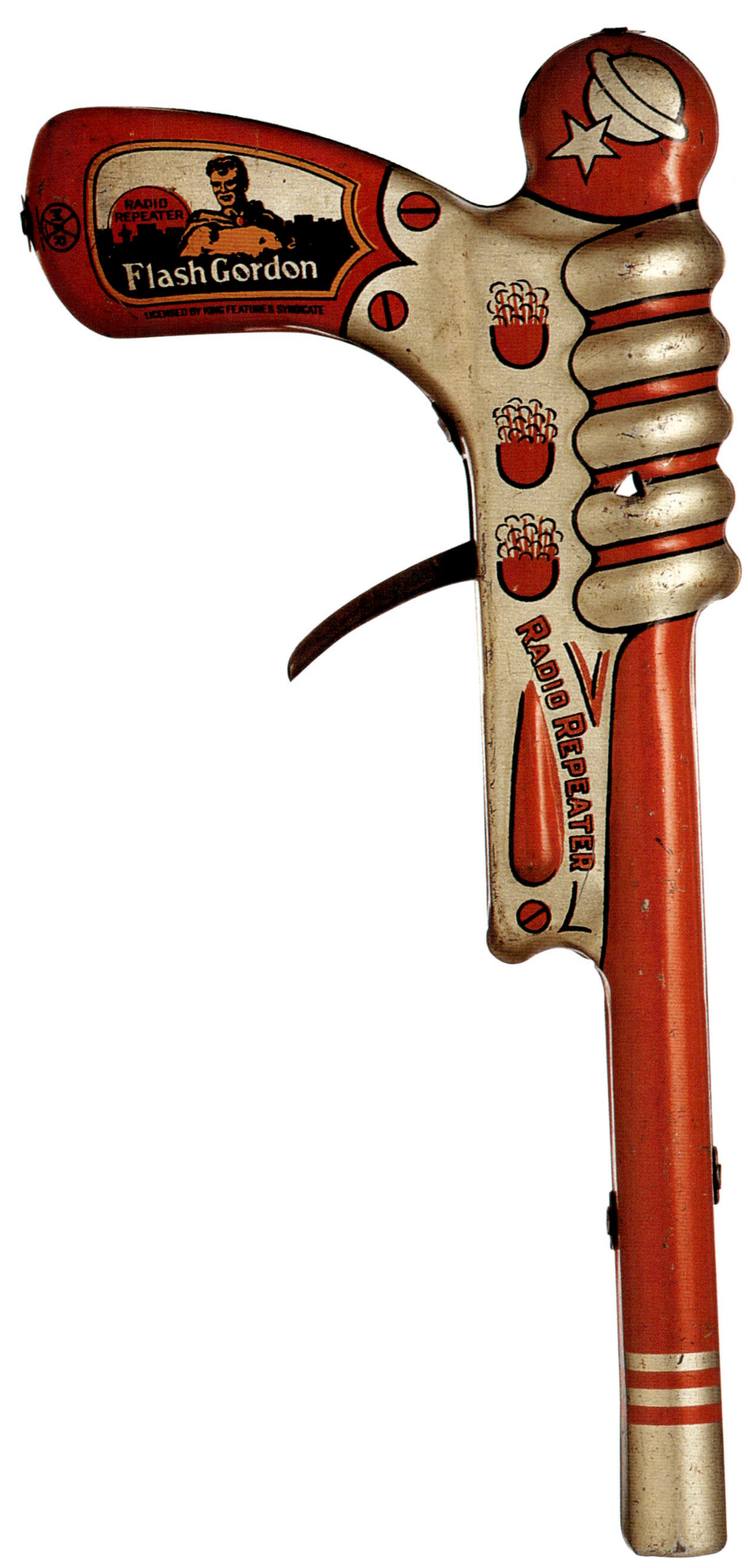

Flash Gordon Radio Repeater, lithographed tin, 4½ x 10 in., Louis Marx Co., U.S.A. mid 1930s

Nu-Matic Paper Popper, pressed steel, 6 x 6½ in., Langson Manufacturing Co., U.S.A. 1930s

Buck Rogers Pop Gun, cardboard, 5½ x 9½ in., Cocomalt, U.S.A. 1933

Buck Rogers Liquid Helium Water Pistol, XZ-44, pressed steel, 5½ x 7¼ in., Daisy Manufacturing Co., U.S.A. 1936

Buck Rogers Holster, 5¼ x 10 in., Daisy Manufacturing Co., U.S.A. 1936, with Disintegrator Pistol

Buck Rogers "Solar Scouts" Radio Club, manual, 5 x 7½ in., Cream of Wheat, U.S.A. 1936

Buck Rogers
25th Century
ROCKET PISTOL
50¢
HERE IT IS!!
A real, line for line copy of Buck Roger's OWN famous Rocket Pistol.
Built of heavy blued gun steel with nickel plated rocket nozzle and back lash deflector.
Has BUCK'S name engraved on every one too.
And does it ZAP . . . say! you can hear it for blocks—a real thriller—no ammunition to buy either.
You can get YOURS at any Daisy Dealer's or department store.
Be a space man—carry a BUCK ROGERS Rocket Pistol.
DAISY MANUFACTURING COMPANY, 230 UNION STREET, PLYMOUTH, MICH.
ABSOLUTELY HARMLESS
MADE BY THE MAKERS OF FAMOUS DAISY AIR RIFLES
Buck Rogers 25th Century Rocket Ship
A FLASHING—ROARING—SPEEDING
model of BUCK ROGERS FAMOUS
INTER-PLANETARY ROCKET CRUISER
MADE FOR
DAISY MANUFACTURING CO
BY
LOUIS MARX and CO., 200 5th AVE., New York, U.S.A.
SAFE
BUCK ROGERS
IN THE 25TH CENTURY

Buck Rogers Rocket Pistol, XZ-31, advertisement, 7 x 10¼ in., Daisy Manufacturing Co., U.S.A. 1934 • Buck Rogers Rocket Ship, box, 4½ x 4½ x 12 in., Louis Marx Co., U.S.A. 1934 • Buck Rogers Origin Storybook, 6 x 8 in., Kellogg's, U.S.A. 1933 • *Buck Rogers Revolt of the Zuggs*, movie poster, 10¾ x 16¼ in., Universal Pictures Corp., U.S.A. 1939 • *Flash Gordon's Trip to Mars*, movie poster, 10½ x 16¾ in., King Features Inc., U.S.A. 1938

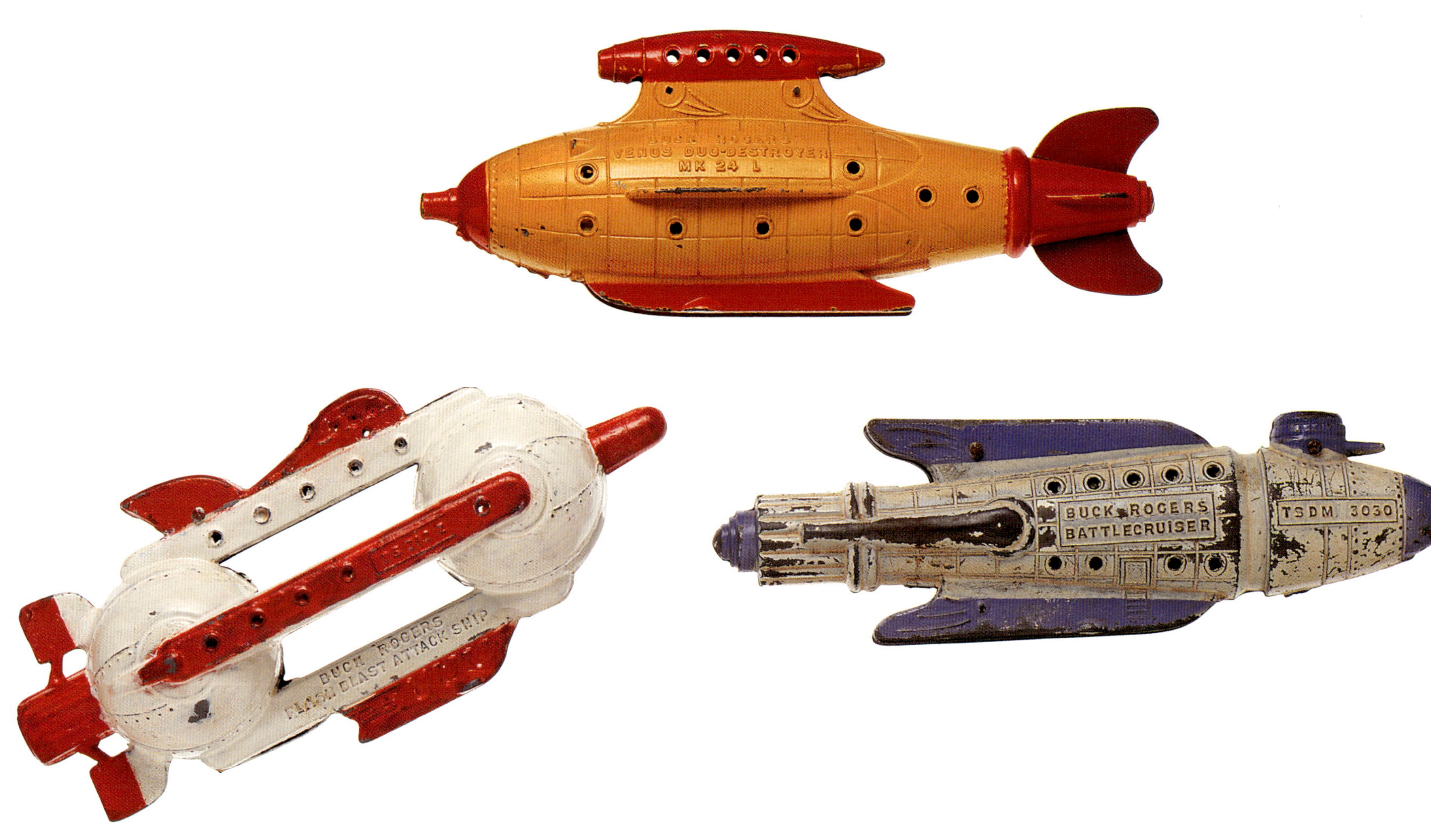

Buck Rogers Tootsie Toy Rocket Ships: Flash Blast Attack Ship (1¾ x 5 in.), Venus Duo-Destroyer (1½ x 4¾ in.), and Battle Cruiser (2 x 4½ in.), Dowst Manufacturing Co., U.S.A. 1937

Buck Rogers Rocket Police Patrol, 4½ x 12 in., Louis Marx Co., U.S.A. 1939

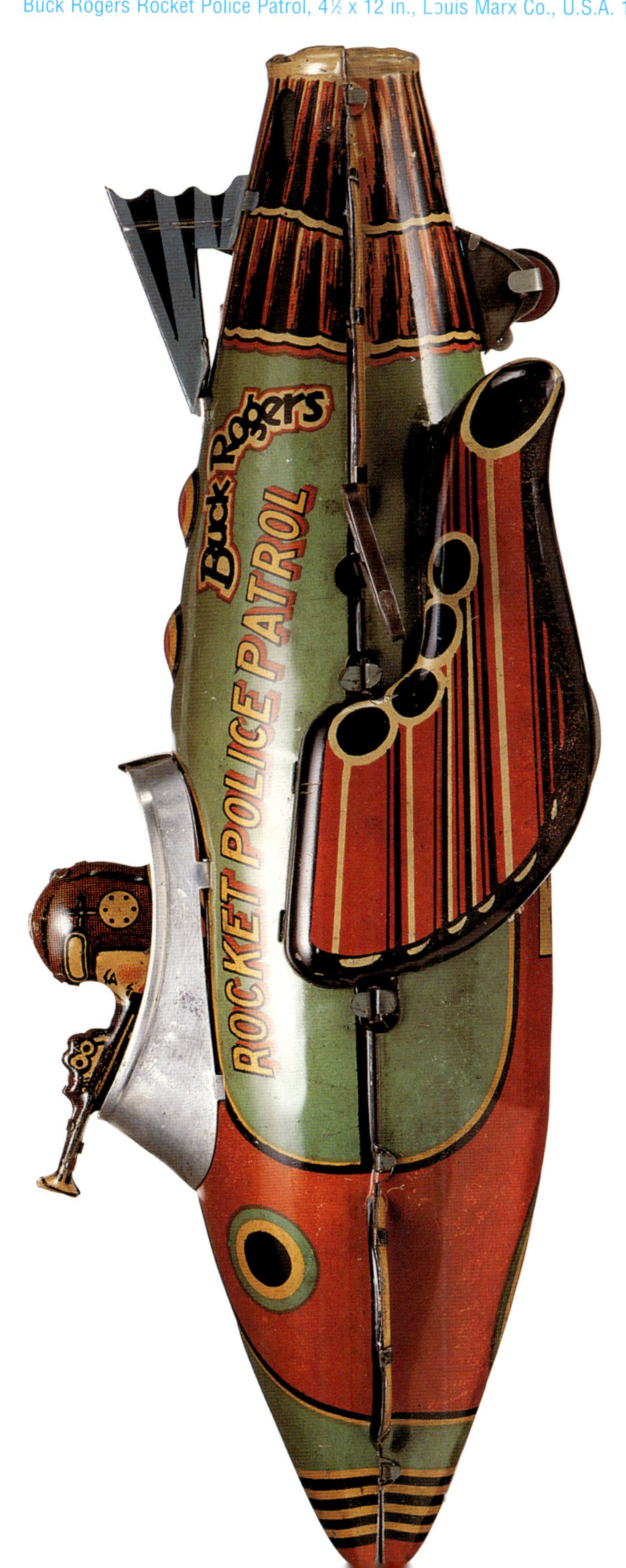

Buck Rogers Helmet, 11 x 24 in., Cocomalt, U.S.A. 1933

Buck Rogers Rocket Ship, 4½ x 12 in., Louis Marx Co., U.S.A. 1934

BUCK ROGERS
ATOMIC PISTOL
U-235
SHOOTS WITH A
BANG AND A FLASH
FISSION RATE INDICATOR
MUZZLE BLAST DEFLECTOR
ATOMIC BEAM DIRECTOR
CONVERGING TARGET FOCUSCOPE
RECOIL ABSORBER
BUCK ROGERS
ATOMIC Pistol
DAISY MFG. CO. PLYMOUTH MICH.
NEUTRON BLAST INITIATOR
WHAT HAPPENS WHEN BUCK ROGERS USES HIS ATOMIC PISTOL
Sight carefully through Atomic Beam Director with right eye, allowing for fluctuating barometric pressure.
Squeeze the Neutron Blast Initiator. This liberates a small stream of neutrons from the Uranium Concentrating Magazine. This discharge is indicated by a brilliant flash from the Fission Rate Indicator, and is controlled in intensity by the Fission Control Governor.
The released stream of neutrons enters the Atomic Power Release Chamber where it bombards the atoms of a secret element, resulting in a controlled chain reaction and a release of atomic energy. This energy flashes out through the Converging Target Focuscope as an invisible and extremely radio-active ray which destroys all evil matter in its path and range.
The Muzzle Blast Deflector prevents any stray energy from shooting back toward the Atomic Pistol user. The Recoil Absorber absorbs all "kick" resulting from release of tremendous energy developed by Atomic Pistol. The loud report is caused by the high velocity rush of air filling the vacuum created by the burst of atomic energy which destroys all air in its path.

Buck Rogers Atomic Pistol, U-235, box (back panel), 1¾ x 6 x 9¾ in., Daisy Manufacturing Co., U.S.A. 1947 • Buck Rogers Atomic Pistol, U-235, advertisement, 7¾ x 9¼ in., Daisy Manufacturing Co., U.S.A. 1947

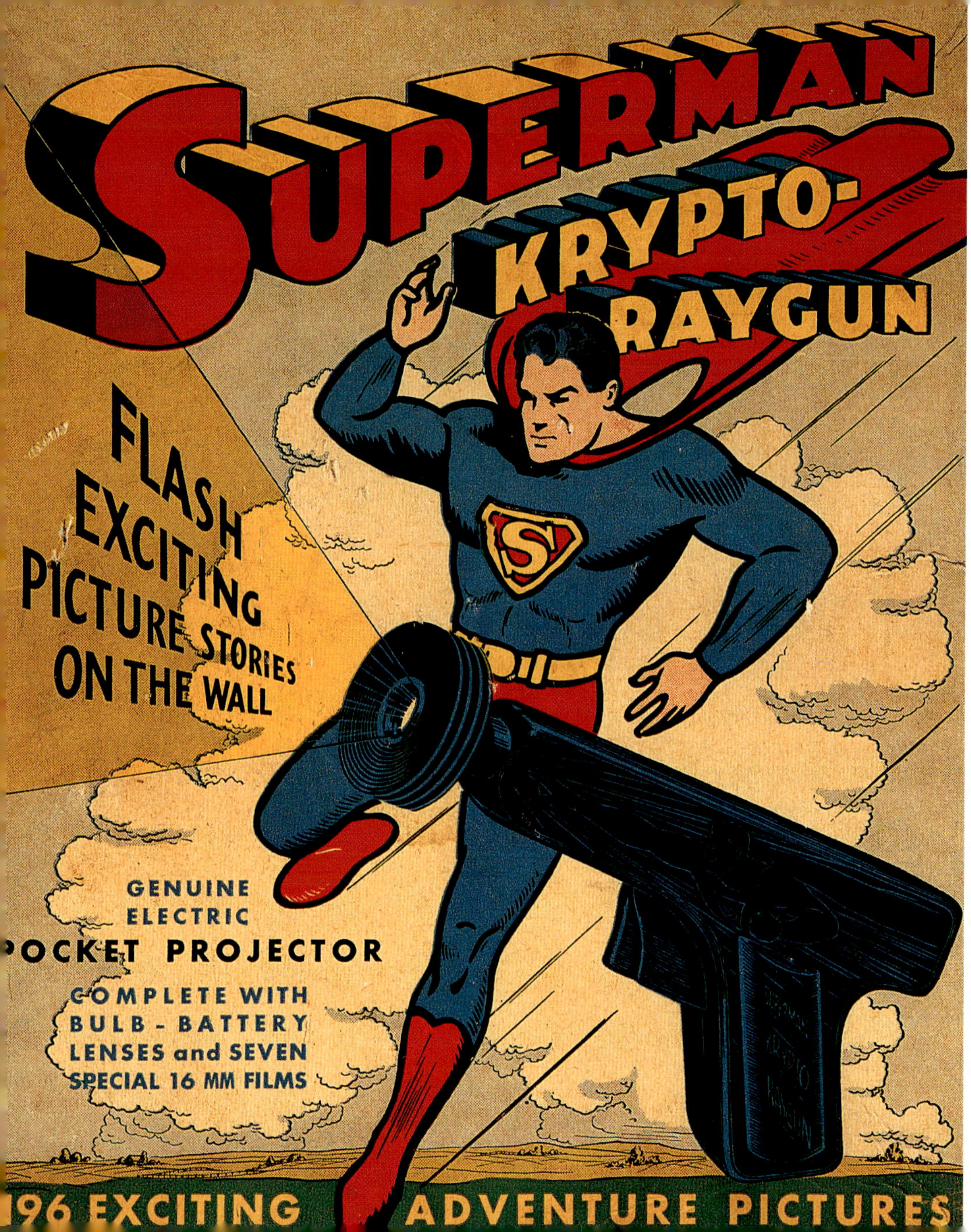

Superman Krypto-Ray Gun Projector Pistol, box, 1¾ x 8¼ x 10¼ in., Daisy Manufacturing Co., U.S.A. 1940

ZZ Pop Ray Gun, pressed steel, 4½ x 7 in., Wyandotte (All Metal Products) Co., U.S.A. early 1940s

Superman Krypto-Ray Gun Projector Pistol, pressed steel, 4 x 7 in., Daisy Manufacturing Co., U.S.A. 1940

Space Gun, die-cast metal with rubber bulb handle, 3 x 7½ in., maker unknown, U.S.A. late 1940s

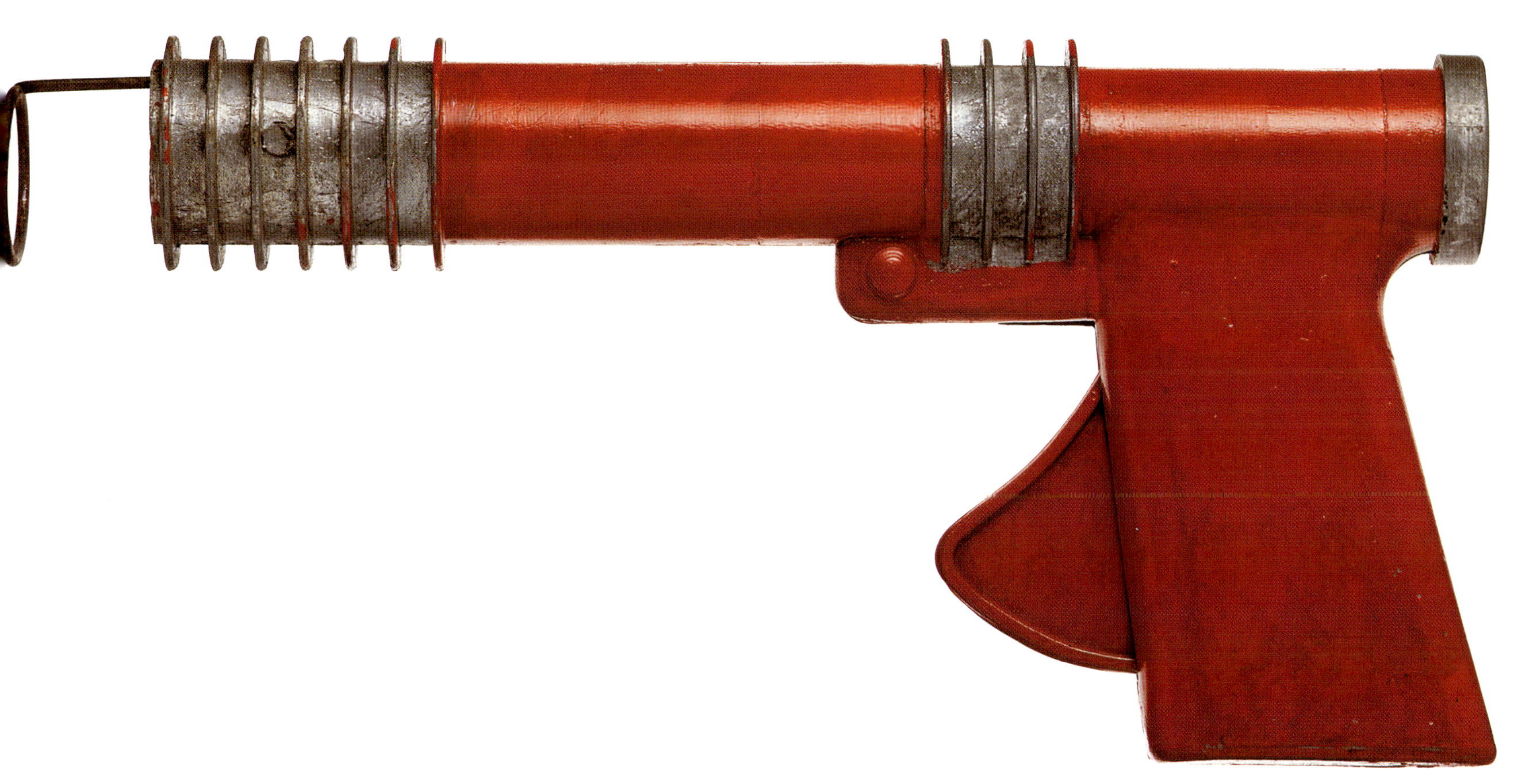

Atom Bubble and Water Gun, die-cast metal, 3½ x 7¼ in., Flyrite Products Inc., U.S.A. late 1940s

ATOM RAY GUN
HILLER

Spinray Blast Pistol, cast aluminum with tin propeller, $4\frac{3}{4} \times 6\frac{1}{2}$ in., Armstrong and Brewer, U.S.A. late 1940s

Atom-Matic Water Rocket Gun, cast aluminum, brass, and plastic, 4½ x 7 in., The Playcraft Co., U.S.A. late 1940s

Prototype Model #1022, plastic, 6 x 10 in., Louis Marx Co., Erie Factory, U.S.A. 1949

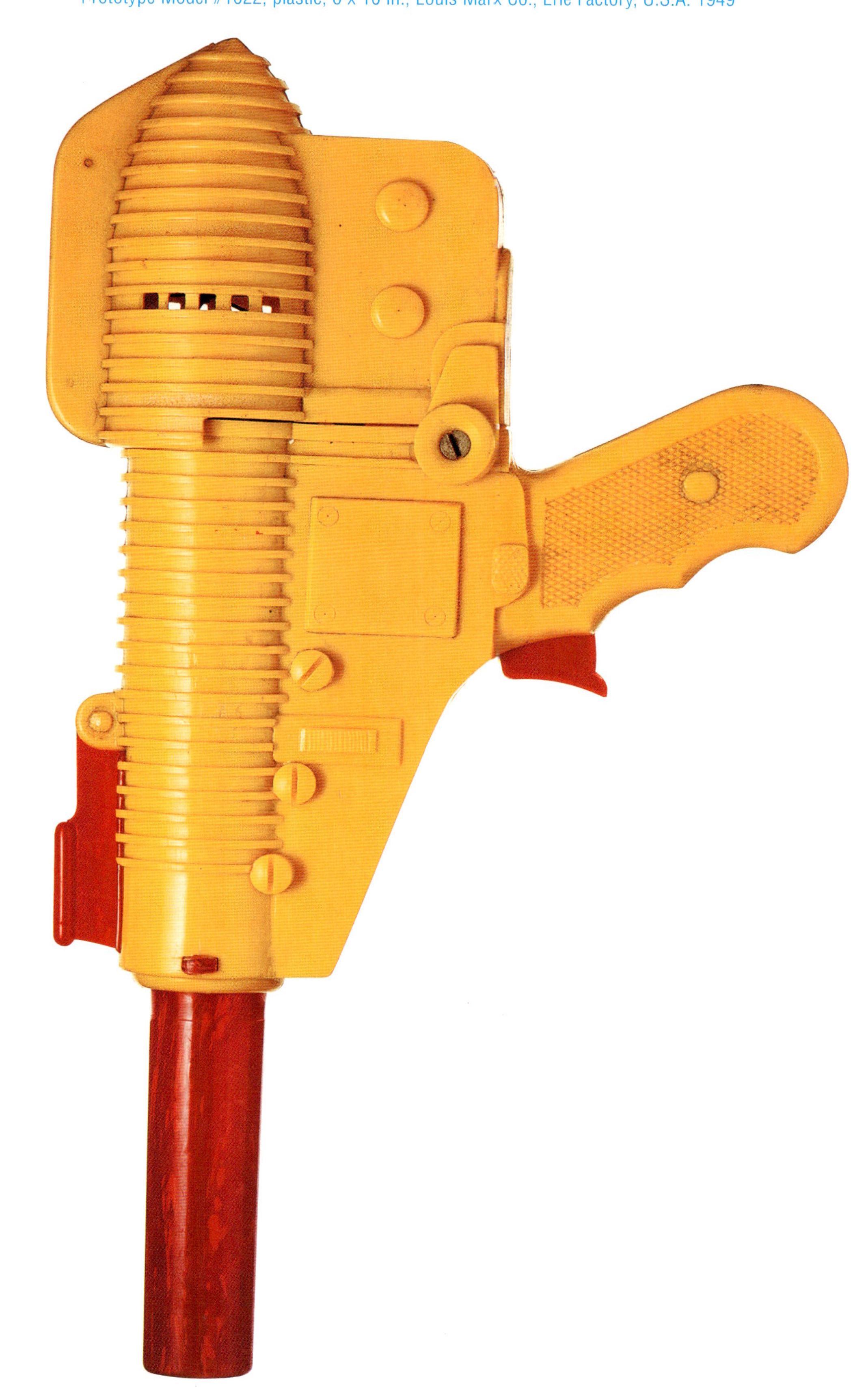

featuring LANCE LEWIS, Space Detective
No. 5
STARTLING COMICS
10¢
A REPUBLIC SERIAL IN 12 CHAPTERS
KING OF THE ROCKET MEN
featuring
TRISTRAM COFFIN · MAE CLARKE
HOUSE PETERS, JR. · DON HAGGERTY
I. STANFORD JOLLEY
Directed by FRED BRANNON

Buck Rogers, badges and buttons (diameters from ¾ to 2¼ in.), U.S.A. 1930s through 1950s

Buck Rogers Space Ranger Helmet, circumference 7½ x 11 in., Sylvania Electric Products, U.S.A. 1952

Buck Rogers Space Ranger Gun, cardboard, 5 x 8 in., Sylvania Electric Products, U.S.A. 1952

Buck Rogers Super Sonic Ray Gun, plastic, 4¾ x 7¾ in., Norton-Honer Mfg. Co., U.S.A. late 1950s

Space Patrol Smoke Gun, plastic, 3½ x 6 in., U.S. Plastics Corp., U.S.A. mid 1950s

Radar Gun, plastic, 4¾ x 6¼ in., maker unknown, U.S.A. 1950s

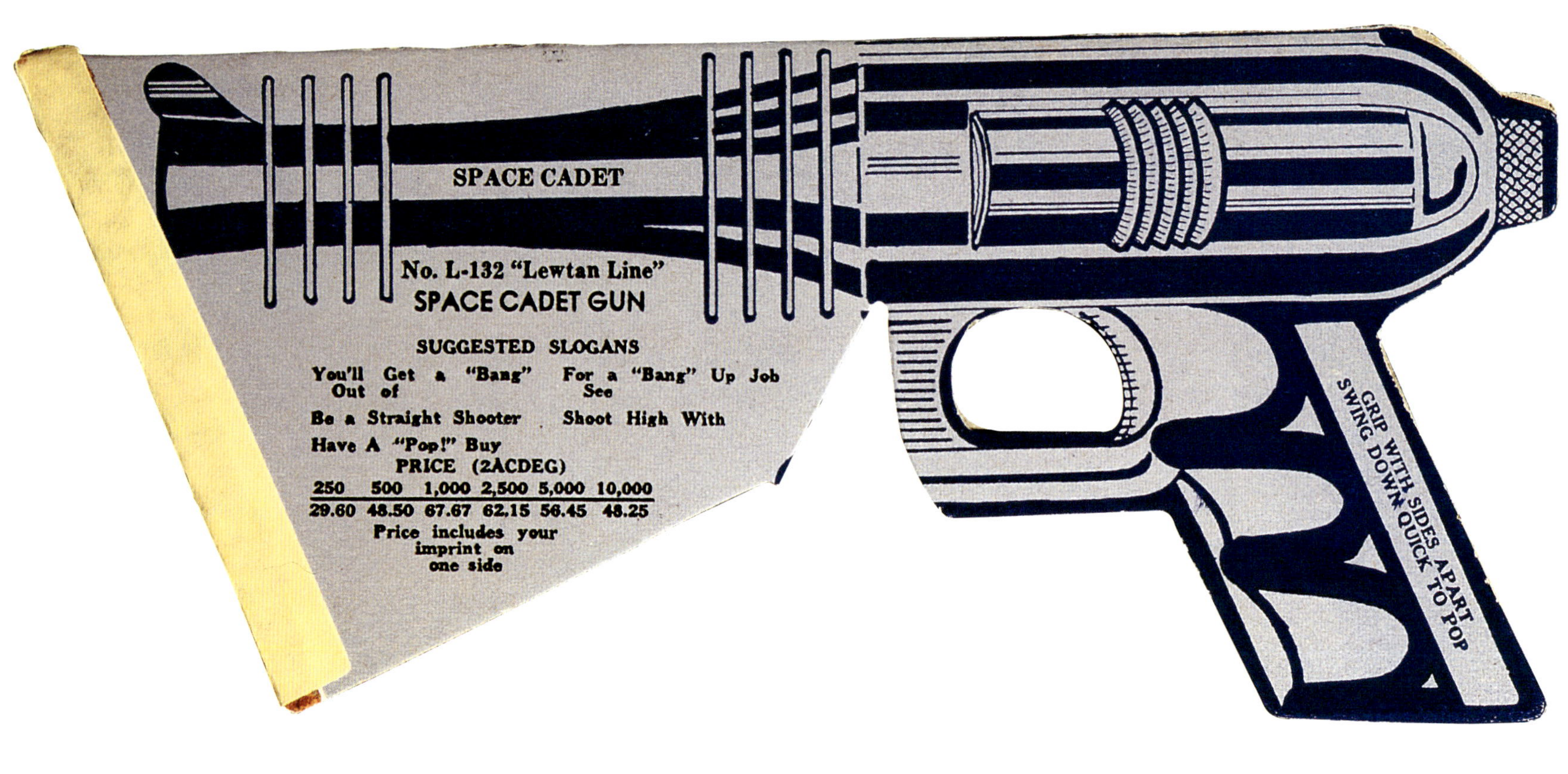
SPACE CADET
No. L-132 "Lewtan Line"
SPACE CADET GUN
SUGGESTED SLOGANS
You'll Get a "Bang" Out of
For a "Bang" Up Job See
Be a Straight Shooter
Shoot High With
Have A "Pop!" Buy
PRICE (2ACDEG)
250 500 1,000 2,500 5,000 10,000
29.60 48.50 67.67 62.15 56.45 48.25
Price includes your imprint on one side
GRIP WITH SIDES APART
SWING DOWN QUICK TO POP

Automatic Repeating Bubble Shooting Gun, plastic, 5½ x 3 in., Arliss Co., Inc., U.S.A. 1950s

NEUTRON
BLASTER
S

Strato Gun, die-cast metal, 4½ x 9¼ in., Futuristic Products Co., U.S.A. mid 1950s

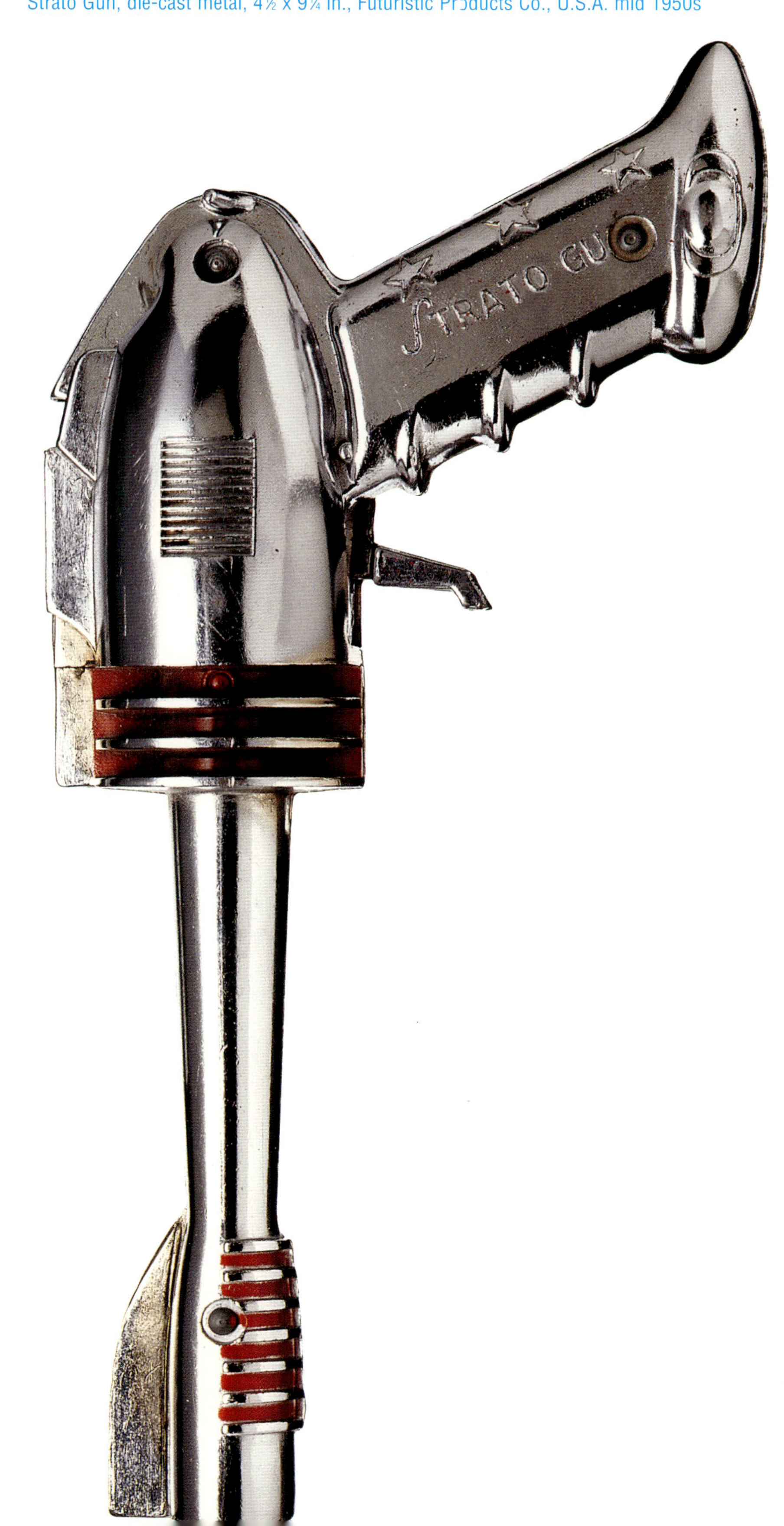

Rocket Dart Pistol, pressed steel, 5½ x 7 in., Daisy Manufacturing Co., U.S.A. early 1950s

DAISY
ZOOKA POP PISTOL
DAISY MFG. CO., PLYMOUTH, MICH. U.S.A.
IT'S A DAISY PLAY GUN

Space Gun, plastic, 3 x 5 in., Palmer Plastics, U.S.A. 1953

Planet Jet, plastic, 3¾ x 5¾ in., Renwal Manufacturing Co., U.S.A. mid 1950s

Martian "Guided Whistle" Bloon-Rocket with Jet-Blast Bloon-Gun, plastic, 5 x 9½ in., Mercury Plastics Corporation, U.S.A. 1950s

Sky Gun, plastic, 4 x 5 in., Propello Toys, U.S.A. 1950s

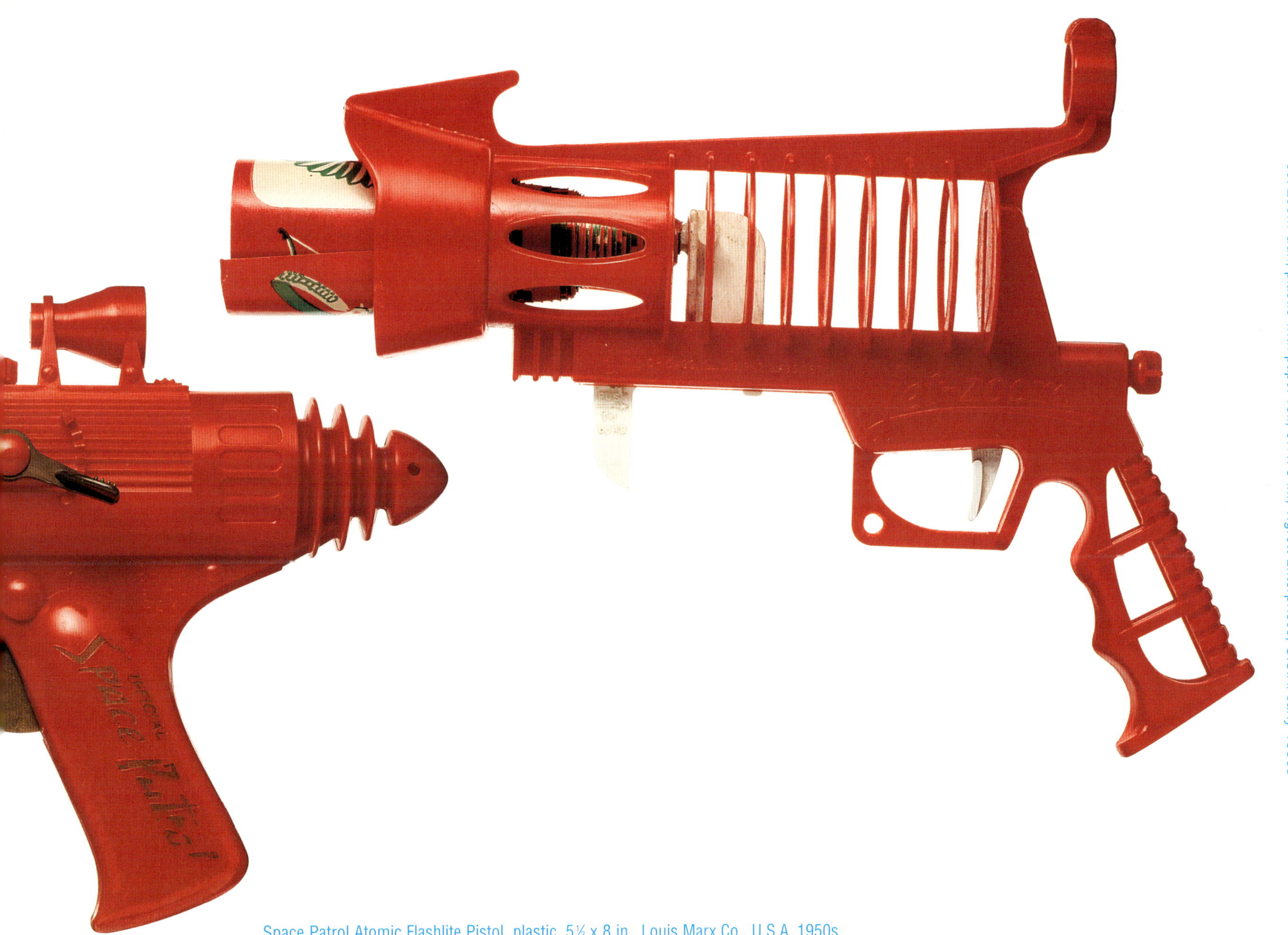

Jet Zoom Gun, plastic with paper roll, 6¾ x 9 in., Tigrett Enterprises, U.S.A. early 1950s

Space Patrol Atomic Flashlite Pistol, plastic, 5½ x 8 in., Louis Marx Co., U.S.A. 1950s

THE ATOMIC WATER PISTOL
Guaranteed to ATOMISE all SPACE INVADERS

Capt. Space BUB·L·ROCKET
TRADE MARK
Blows BIG bubbles, LITTLE bubble
S·T·R·E·A·M·S of bubbles,
GALAXIES of bubbles -
WITHOUT REFUELING!
Load it with any regular
AUTOMATIC FEED!

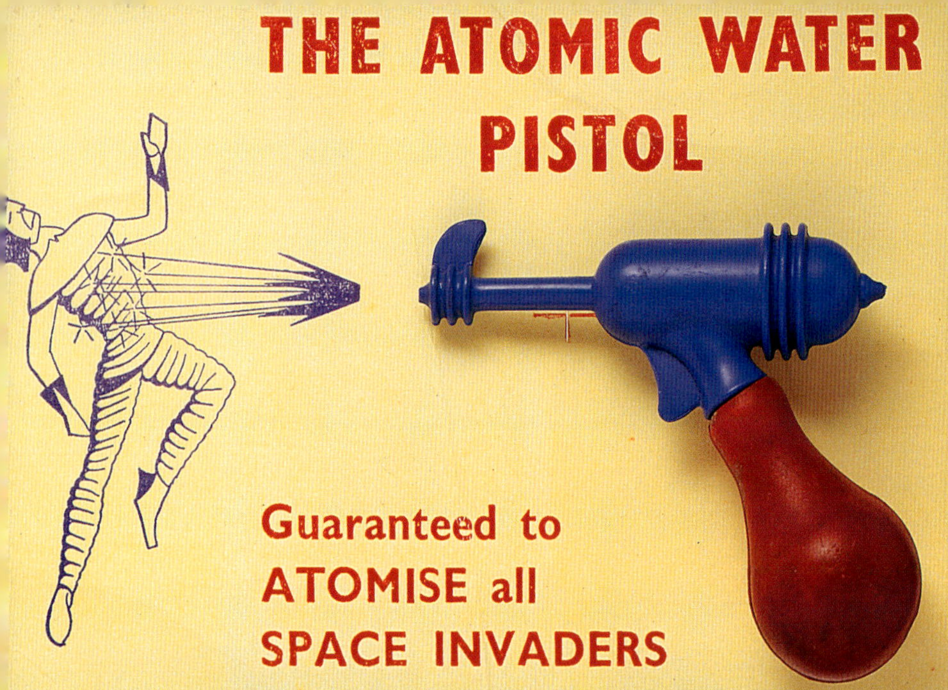

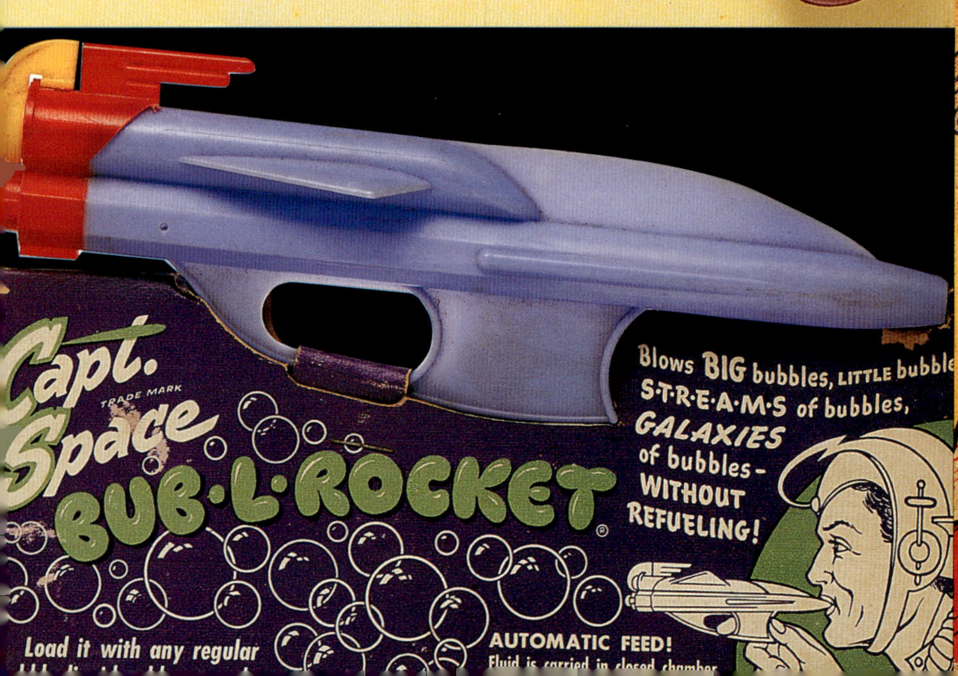

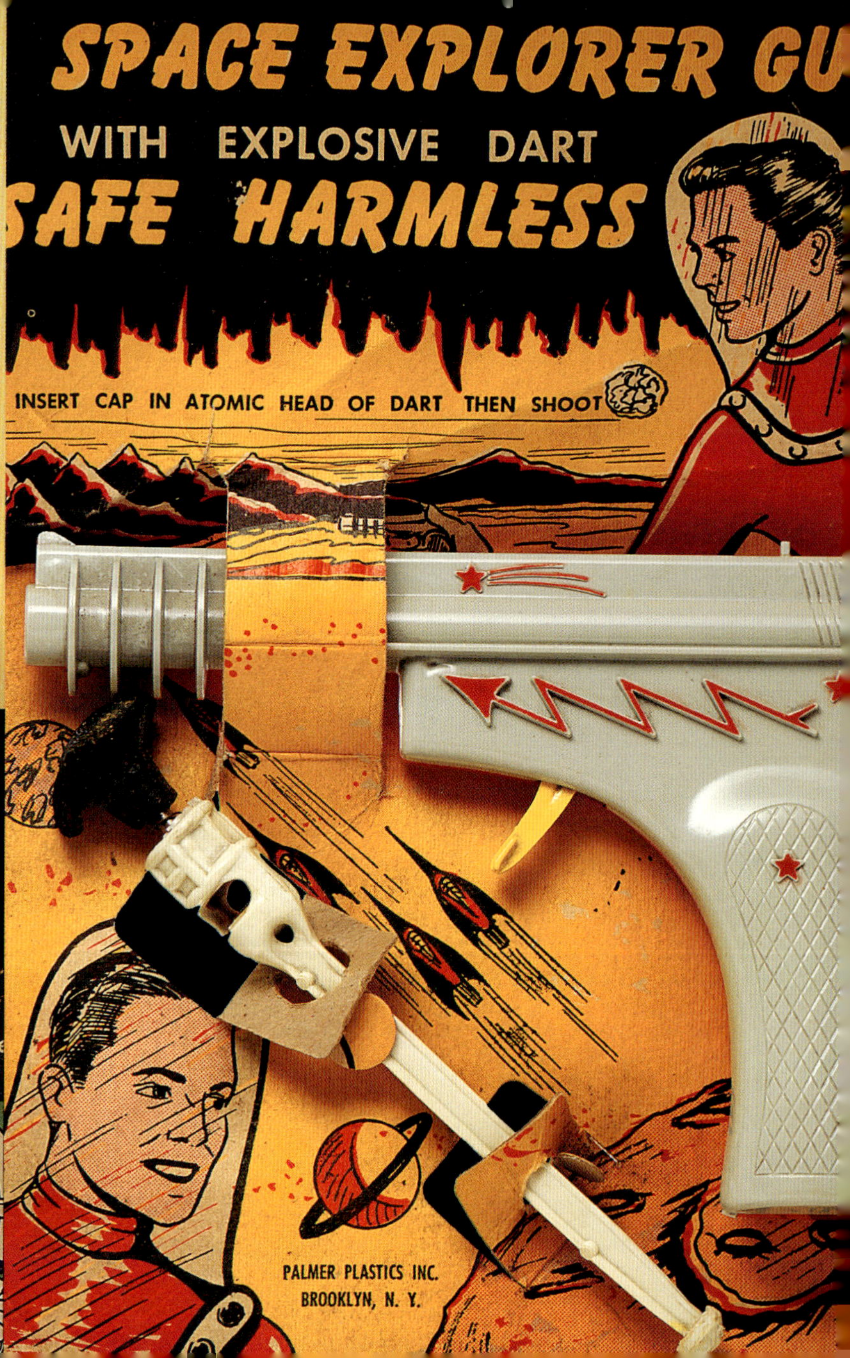
SPACE EXPLORER GU
WITH EXPLOSIVE DART
SAFE HARMLESS
INSERT CAP IN ATOMIC HEAD OF DART THEN SHOOT
PALMER PLASTICS INC.
BROOKLYN, N. Y.

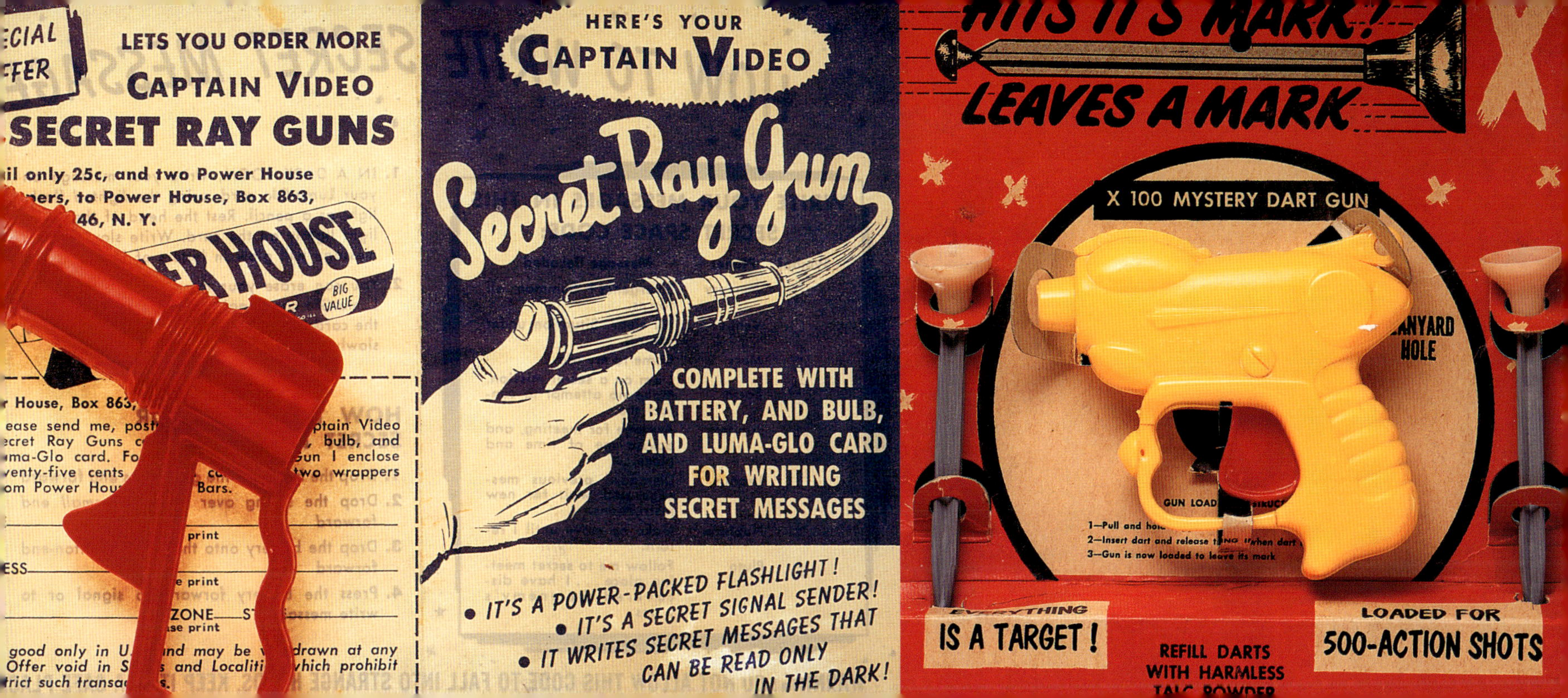

LETS YOU ORDER MORE
CAPTAIN VIDEO
SECRET RAY GUNS

HERE'S YOUR
CAPTAIN VIDEO
Secret Ray Gun
COMPLETE WITH BATTERY, AND BULB, AND LUMA-GLO CARD FOR WRITING SECRET MESSAGES
• IT'S A POWER-PACKED FLASHLIGHT!
• IT'S A SECRET SIGNAL SENDER!
• IT WRITES SECRET MESSAGES THAT CAN BE READ ONLY IN THE DARK!

LEAVES A MARK
X 100 MYSTERY DART GUN
IS A TARGET !
LOADED FOR
500-ACTION SHOTS
REFILL DARTS
WITH HARMLESS

Smoke Ring Gun, plastic, 6 x 9 in., Nu-Age Products Inc., U.S.A. early 1950s

Whistle Gun, plastic, 2¾ x 4¾ in., maker unknown, U.S.A. 1950s

Space Gun, plastic, 2 x 4½ in., Thomas Co., U.S.A. 1950s

Space Patrol Rocket Dart Gun, plastic, 5¼ x 9¾ in., U.S. Plastics Co., U.S.A. 1954

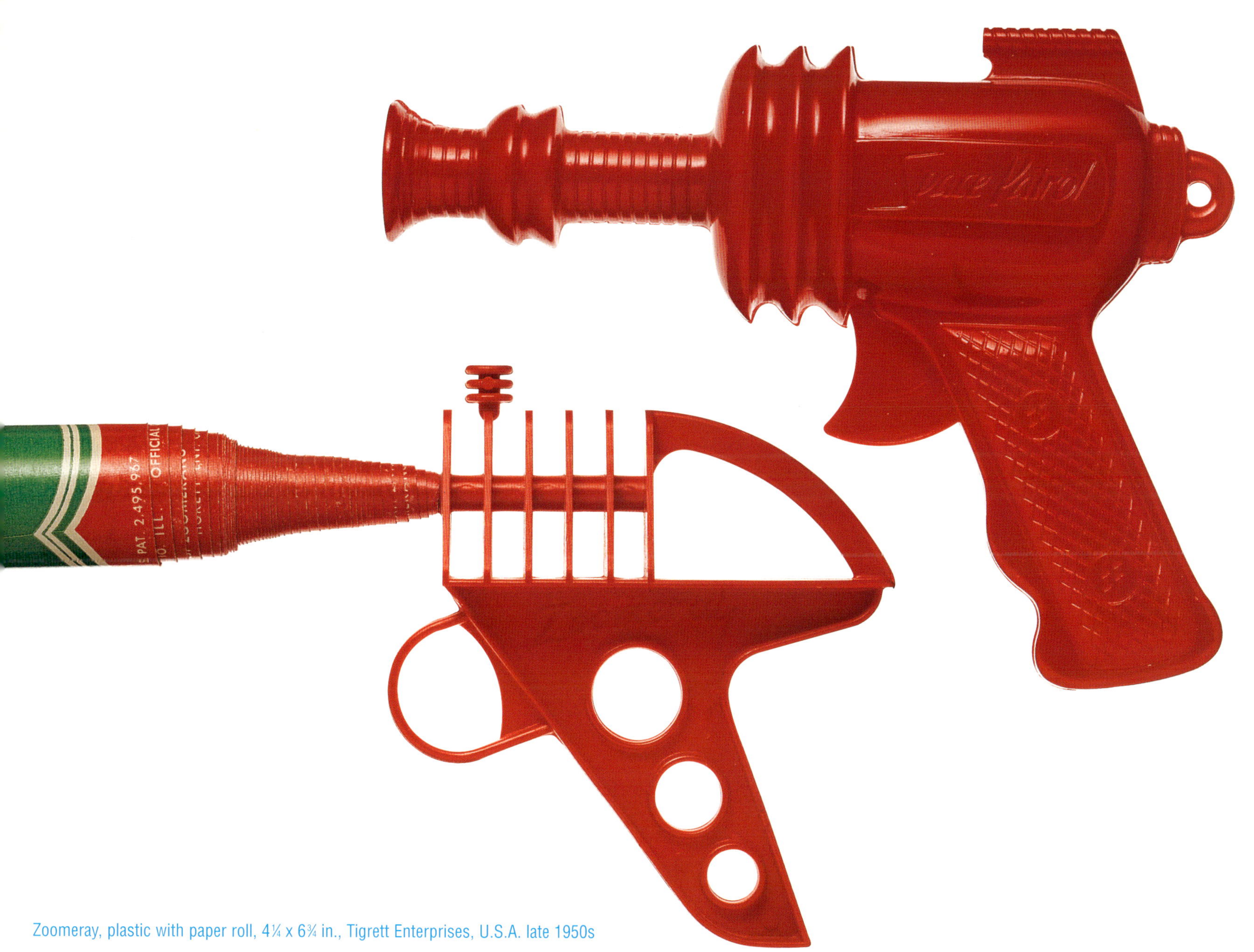

Space Patrol Cosmic Smoke Gun, plastic, 3½ x 4½ in., U.S. Plastics Co., U.S.A. 1952

Zoomeray, plastic with paper roll, 4¼ x 6¾ in., Tigrett Enterprises, U.S.A. late 1950s

Atomic Pistol, tin and plastic, 4¼ x 7½ in., T.N., Japan late 1950s

Atomic Flash Gun, pressed steel, 5 x 7½ in., J Chein & Co., U.S.A. mid 1950s

Space Pistol, lithographed tin with plastic propeller, 5 x 7¾ in., T.N., Japan late 1950s

888 Space Gun, lithographed tin, 2½ x 3 in., maker unknown, Japan 1950s

Space Control Gun, lithographed tin, 3 x 3¾ in., T.N., Japan 1950s

DIA Space Gun, lithographed tin, 3 x 4 in., maker unknown, Japan 1950s

Atomic Jet-Gun, cast aluminum, 4 x 6 in., Crescent Toys, England 1950s

Space Pilot Missile Gun, plastic, 6 x 9 in., Merit, England 1950s

Space Pilot Super-Sonic Gun, plastic, 4½ x 8¾ in., Merit, England 1950s

Prototype Model #1942-A, plastic, 4½ x 7½ in., Louis Marx Co., Girard Factory, U.S.A. 1952

Prototype Model #1944, plastic, 4 x 6¾ in., Louis Marx Co., Girard Factory, U.S.A. 1952

Prototype Model #1843, plastic, 4¼ x 7 in., Louis Marx Co., Girard Factory, U.S.A. 1952

Space Squadron Sonic Beam Gun, plastic, 4½ x 7¼ in., Lone Star, England 1950s

Prototype Rex Mars Planet Patrol Rifle, plastic and tin, 7 x 26 in., Louis Marx Co., U.S.A. early 1950s

Tommy Ray, plastic, 7 x 23 in., B & W Molded Plastics, U.S.A. 1950s

Space Ship Water Guns, die-cast metal with rubber bulbs, 2 x 3 in., maker unknown, England 1950s

JET JR
S

Atomic Jet Gun, die-cast metal, 4½ x 7¾ in., The J. & E. Stevens Co., U.S.A. early 1950s

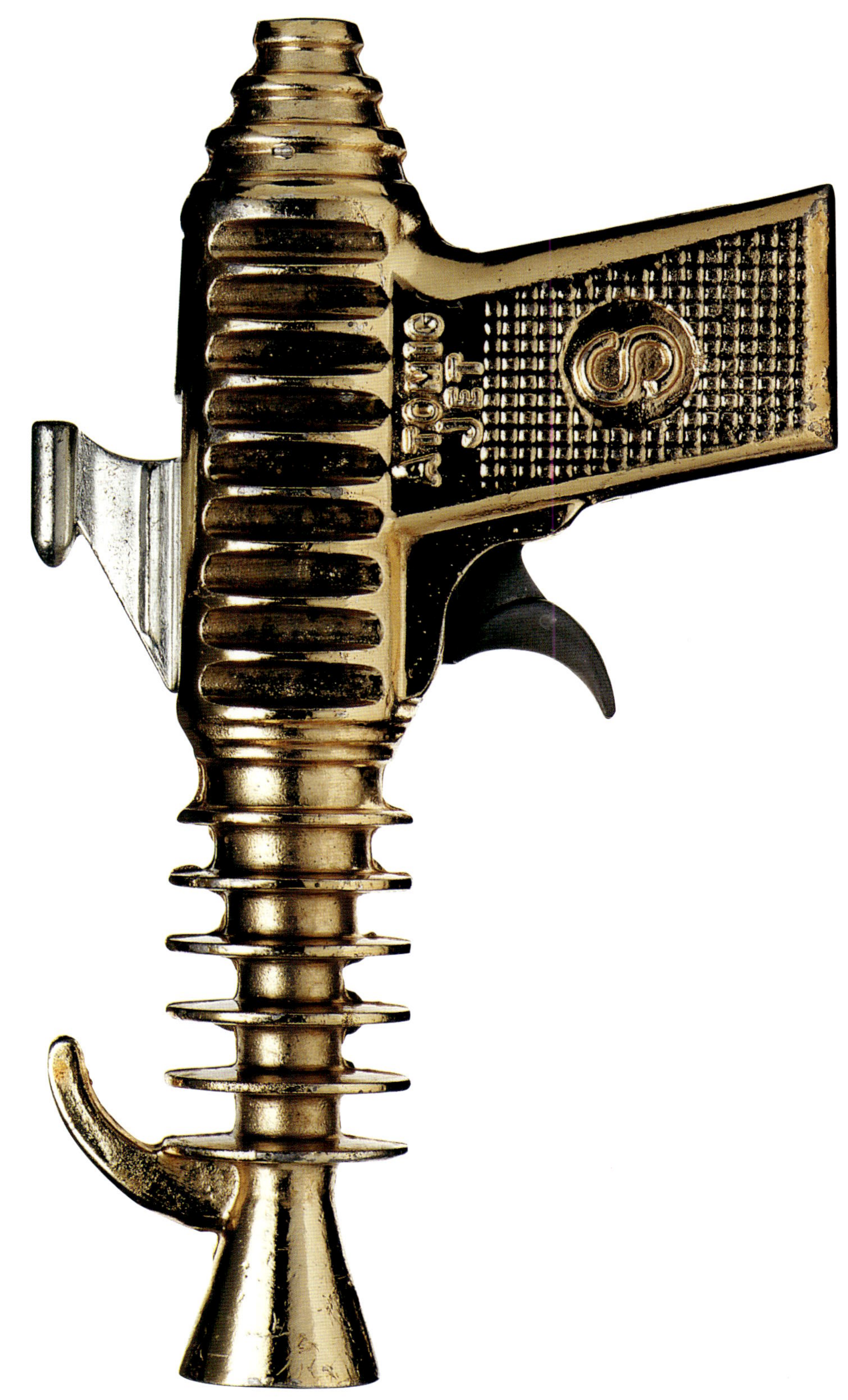

Space Gun, lithographed tin, 3 x 3½ in., maker unknown, Japan 1950s

Cowboy Space Gun, lithographed tin, 3¼ x 4 in., F.G., Japan 1950s

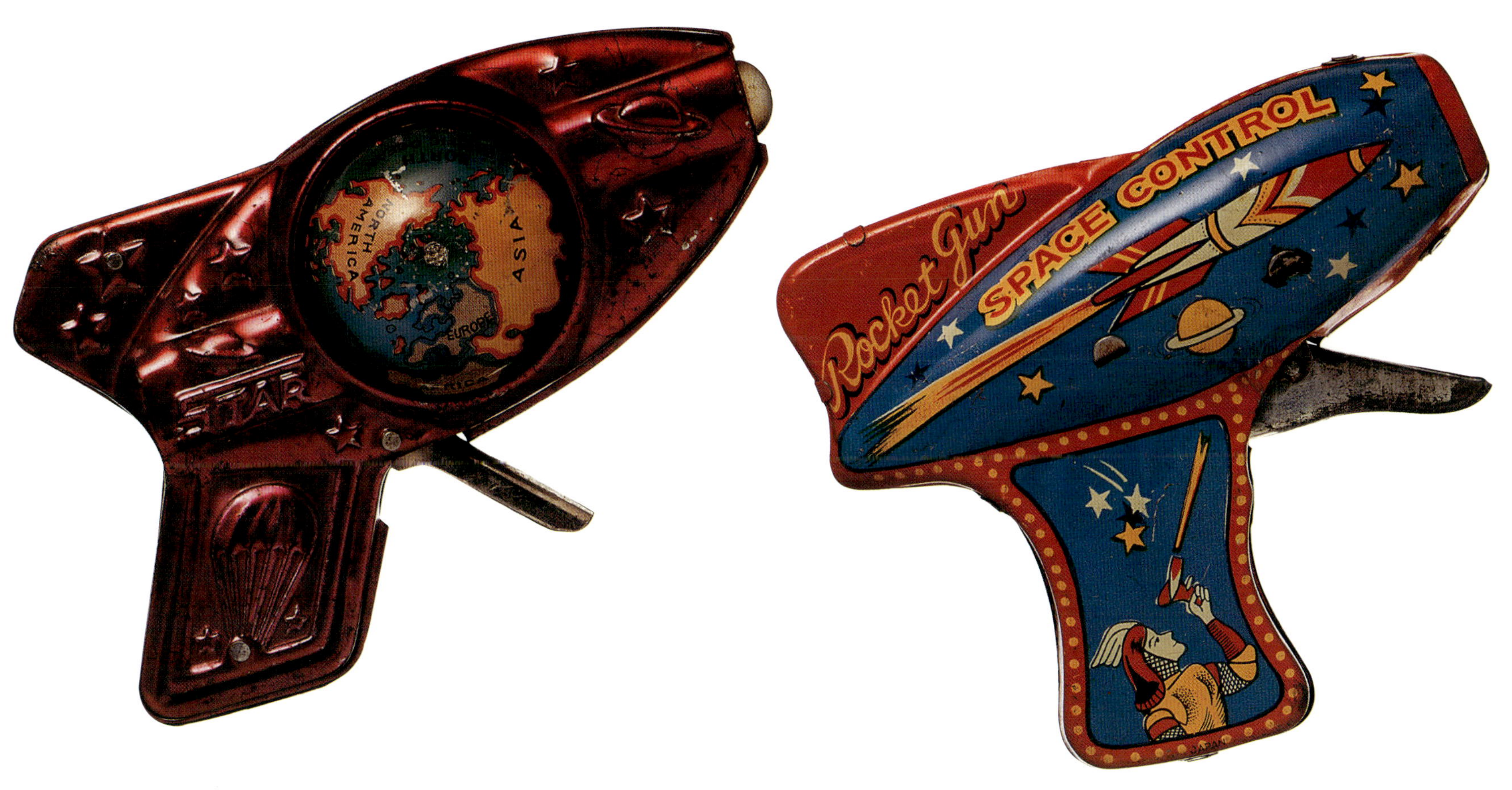

Star Globe Water Gun, painted and lithographed tin, 3 x 4½ in., maker unknown, Japan 1950s

Space Control Rocket Gun, lithographed tin, 3½ x 4 in., maker unknown, Japan 1950s

SPARKLING

Special

Pistol

F.6
JAPAN

Cowboy Space Gun, box, 1 x 3¼ x 4 in., F.G., Japan 1950s
Flash Gordon Puzzle, 10¼ x 14½ in., Milton Bradley, U.S.A. 1951

ASH GORDON
MB
MILTON BRADLEY
4216-X-2
FEBRUARY
25¢
CAN EARTH REPEL AN ALIEN INVADER?
A ZIFF DAVIS PUBLICATION
AMAZING
ANC
STORIES
THE IRON MEN OF VENUS
By
DON WILCOX

Dan Dare Planet Gun, plastic, 3¾ x 4¼ in., and box, 2 x 7 x 11 in., Merit, England 1950s

DAN DARE
PLANET GUN
DAN DARE
PLANET GUN
WITH 3 SHOCKPROOF SPINNING MISSILES
RANDALL LTD

Pyrotomic Disintegrator, plastic, 5½ x 9 in., Pyro Plastics Corp., U.S.A. 1950s

3-Way Futurama Ray Gun, plastic, 5 x 9 in., Ideal Toy Corp., U.S.A. 1951

Rex Mars Planet Patrol Sparking Pistol, plastic, 5¼ x 6¼ in., Louis Marx Co., U.S.A. 1950s

Ratchet Sound Gun, plastic, 5½ x 7 in., Ideal Toy Corp., U.S.A. 1950s

Space Gun, lithographed tin, 3 x 3½ in., SAN, Japan 1950s

Space Dart Gun, lithographed tin and wood, 3½ x 10½ in., maker unknown, Japan 1950s

Space Gun, lithographed tin, 4 x 5½ in., maker unknown, Japan 1950s

Cap Firing Sub-Machine Gun, plastic, Ideal Toy Corp., U.S.A. 1953

Tom Corbett Space Cadet Atomic Rifle, plastic, 6½ x 24 in., Louis Marx Co., U.S.A. 1950s

Captain Space Solar Scout, plastic, 7 x 26 in., Louis Marx Co., U.S.A. mid 1950s

Flash Gordon Signal Pistol, pressed steel, 5½ x 6½ in., Louis Marx Co., U.S.A. mid 1950s

Atomic Disintegrator, die-cast metal, 5¼ x 7½ in., The Hubley Mfg. Co., U.S.A. 1954 and 1955

Space Gun, lithographed tin, 4½ x 7½ in., Daiya, Japan 1950s

Cosmic Ray Gun, pressed steel, 5 x 8½ in., Ranger Steel Products Corp., U.S.A. mid 1950s

FLASH GORDON
© KING FEATURES SYND.
ARRESTING RAY

Dan Dare Cosmic Ray Gun, plastic, 4¾ x 6¼ in., Palitoy, England 1950s

EARTH VS. THE FLYING SAUCERS

YING SAUCERS ATTACK!

WARNING! TAKE COVER!

STARRING

HUGH MARLOWE · JOAN TAYLOR

WITH DONALD CURTIS

SCREEN PLAY BY
GEORGE WORTHING YATES and RAYMOND T. MARCUS · CURT SIODMAK · RAY HARRYHAUSEN

PRODUCED BY · EXECUTIVE PRODUCER · DIRECTED BY

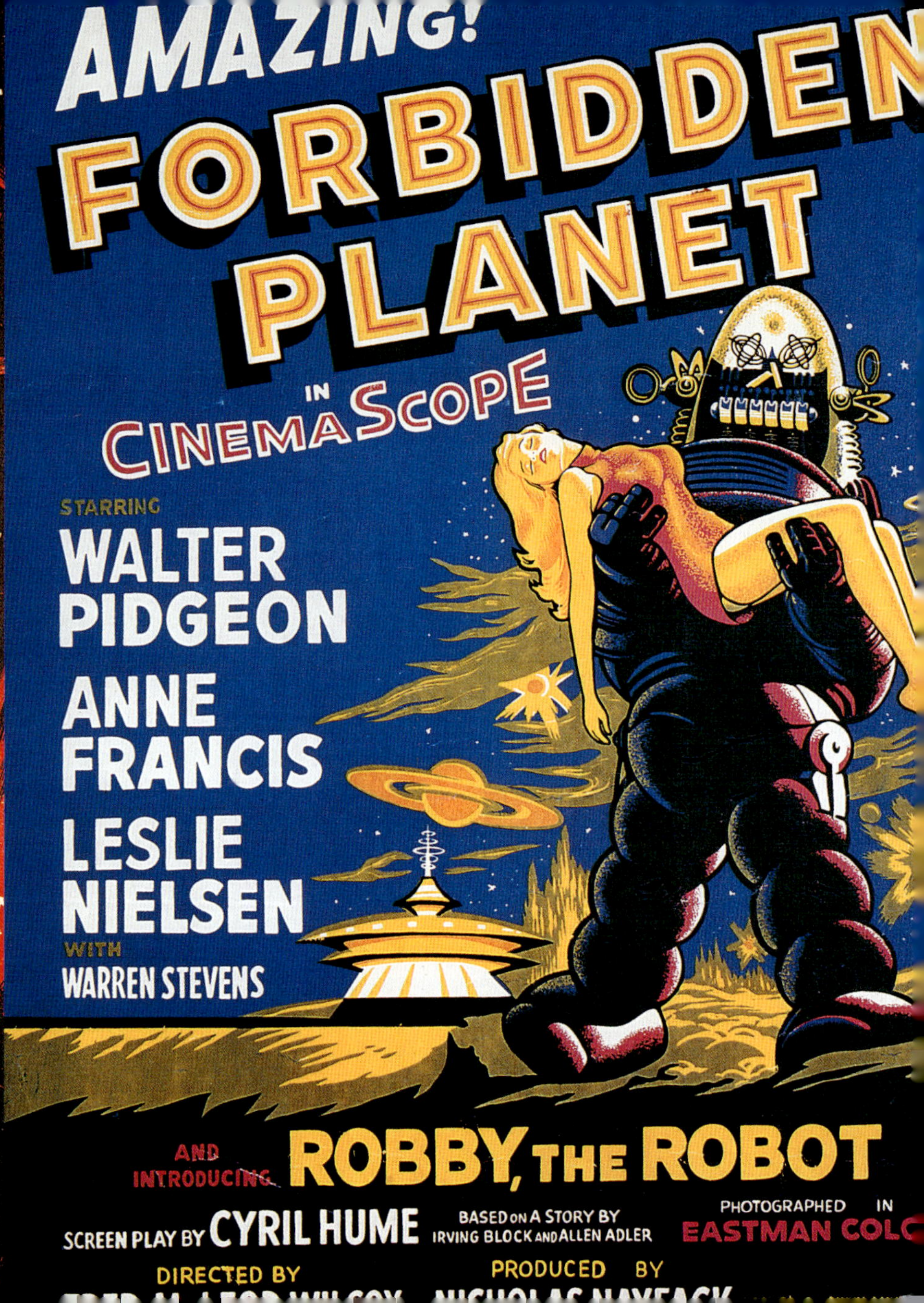

AMAZING!

FORBIDDEN PLANET

IN CINEMASCOPE

STARRING

WALTER PIDGEON

ANNE FRANCIS

LESLIE NIELSEN

WITH

WARREN STEVENS

AND INTRODUCING ROBBY, THE ROBOT

SCREEN PLAY BY CYRIL HUME

BASED ON A STORY BY IRVING BLOCK AND ALLEN ADLER

PHOTOGRAPHED IN EASTMAN COLO

DIRECTED BY

PRODUCED BY

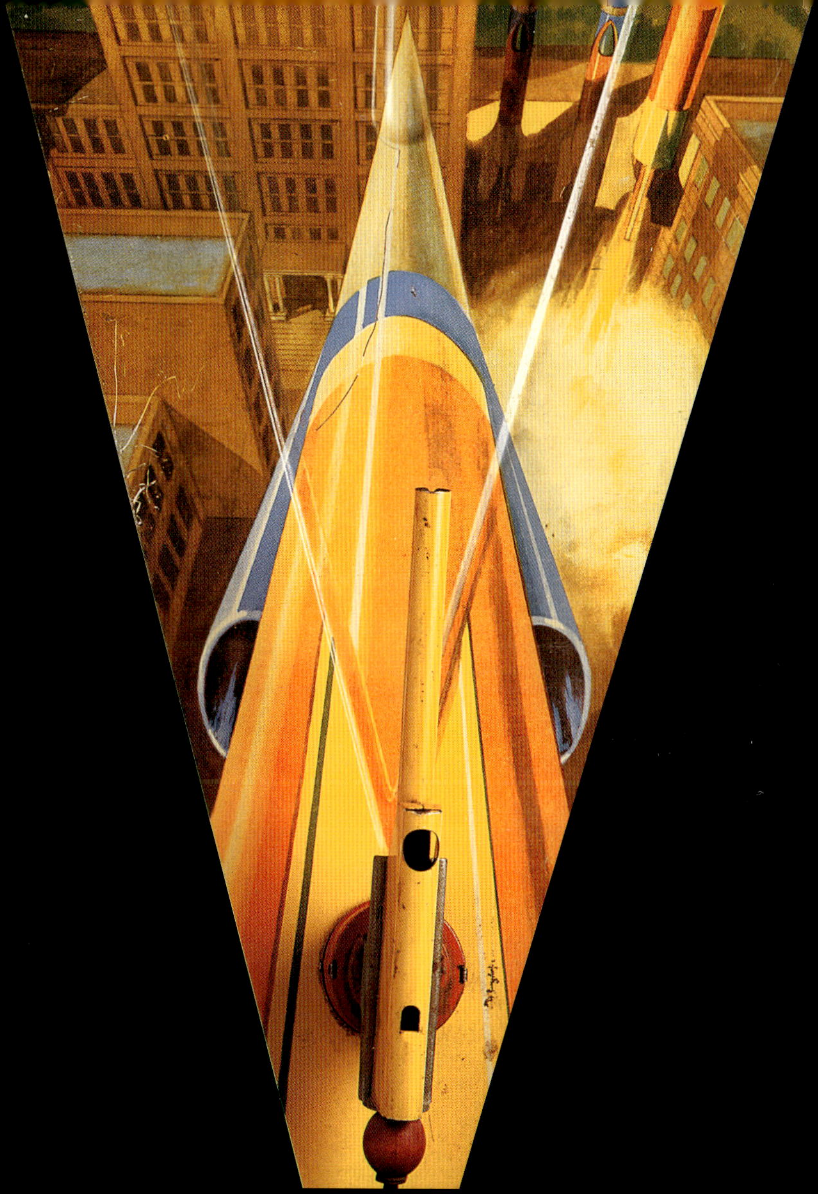

Earth vs. The Flying Saucers, movie poster, 10½ x 16¼ in., Columbia Pictures, U.S.A. 1956
Forbidden Planet, movie poster, 10½ x 14¼ in,. Metro-Goldwyn-Mayer Pictures, U.S.A. 1956
Super Target, game, 15 x 23 in., T. Cohn, U.S.A. early 1950s
Space Shooting Range, 10 x 15½ in., maker unknown, U.S.A. 1950s

YOUR GATEWAY TO SCIENCE-FANTASY WORLDS

Fantastic

ADVENTURES

JANUARY

25¢

The JUSTICE of TOR

THE ROCKET MAN

STARRING

CHARLES COBURN · SPRING BYINGTON · ANNE FRANCI

JOHN AGAR · and GEORGE 'FOGHORN' WINSLOW

WITH

STANLEY CLEMENTS

EMORY PARNELL

JUNE CLAYWORTH

DON HAGGERTY

Fantastic Adventures, magazine cover, 7 x 9½ in., January 1951

The Rocket Man, movie poster, 10¾ x 16½ in., Twentieth Century Fox, U.S.A. 1954

Queen of Outer Space, movie poster, 10¾ x 13½ in., Allied Artists, U.S.A. 1958

QUEEN OF
OUTER SPACE
COLOR BY DE LUXE
CINEMASCOPE
An ALLIED ARTISTS Picture
starring
ZSA ZSA GABOR
ERIC FLEMING · LAURIE MITCHELL · LISA DAVIS

Holster, 5¾ x 9½ in., Halco, U.S.A. 1950s, with Space Patrol Atomic Flashlight Pistol, Louis Marx Co.

Space Pilot Missile Gun, box, 2½ x 7 x 11½ in., Merit, England 1950s

Dan Dare Cosmic Ray Gun, box, 3¼ x 7¼ x 10 in., Palitoy, England 1950s

FLASH GORDON
CLICK RAY
PISTOL

Atomic Gun, lithographed tin and plastic, 4¼ x 8¾ in., Haji, Japan 1960s

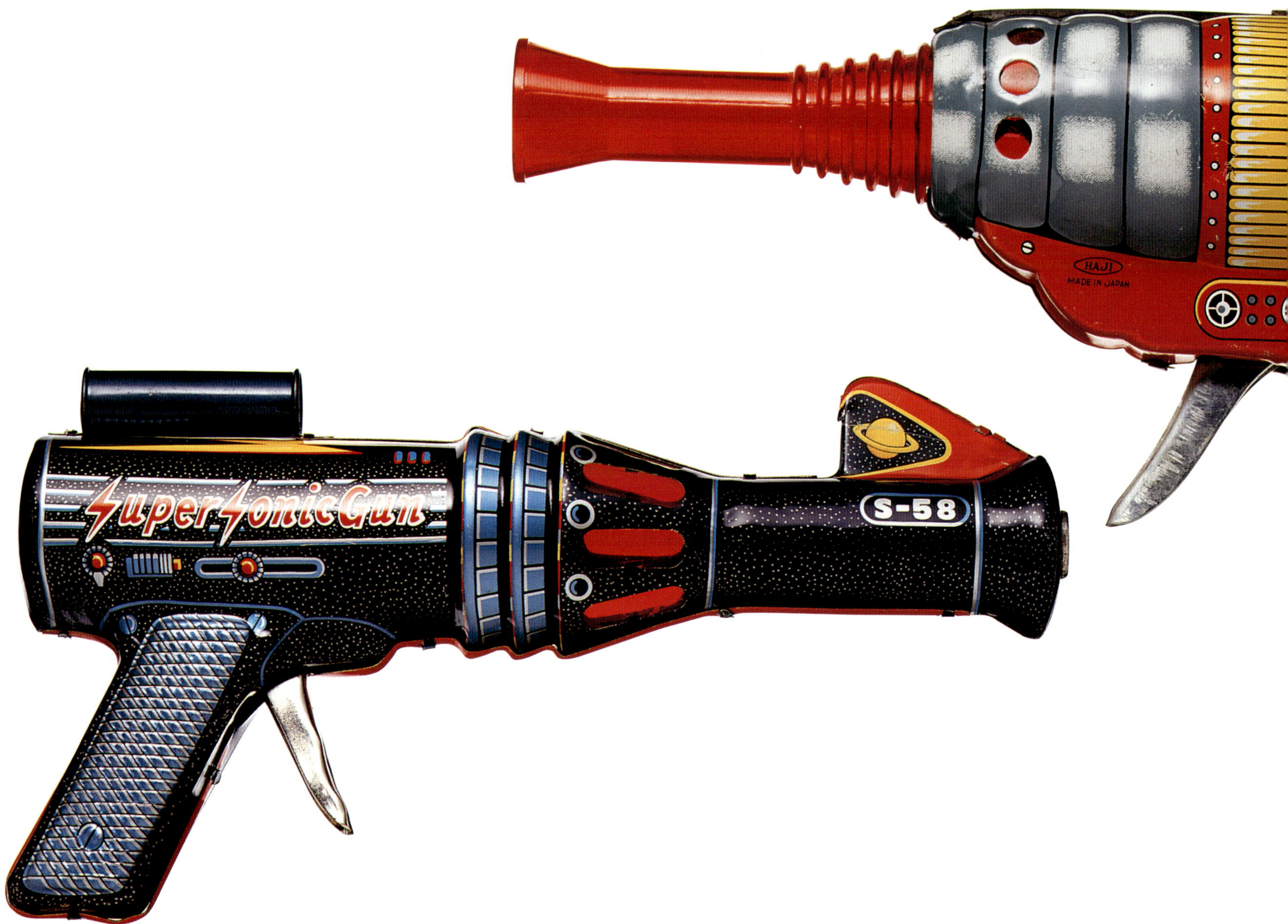

S58 Super Sonic Gun, lithographed tin, 4¾ x 9½ in., Daiya, Japan 1960s

Baby Space Gun, lithographed tin, 3½ x 5¾ in., Daiya, Japan 1960s

Space Gun, lithographed tin and plastic, 5½ x 9 in., maker unknown, Japan 1960s

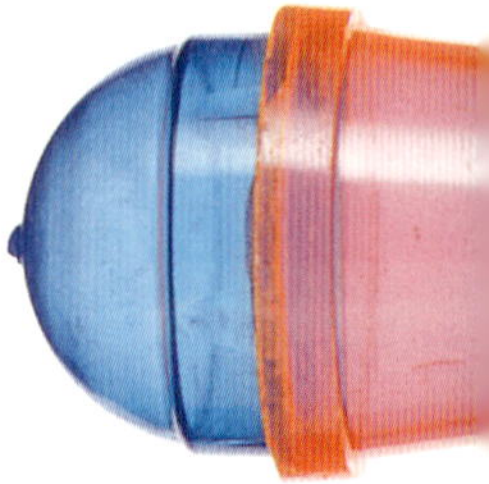

Space Gun, lithographed tin, 4¼ x 7 in., Toy Hero, Japan 1960s

Space Gun 45, lithographed tin and plastic, 4½ x 6¾ in., K.O., Japan 1960s

Space Jet, lithographed tin and plastic, 4½ x 9¾ in., K.O., Japan 1960s

Space Ray Gun, lithographed tin and plastic, 5 x 15 in., K.O., Japan 1960s

Super Sonic Space Gun, lithographed tin, 4 x 7¼ in., Daiya, Japan 1960s

Space Gun, plastic, 6 x 10 in., maker unknown, France 1960s

Space Gun, plastic, 3½ x 4¾ in., Geyper, Spain 1960s

Space Outlaw Gun, die-cast metal, 5½ x 9¾ in., B.C.M., England 1960s

Atomic Space Pistol, lithographed tin and plastic, 5½ x 7 in., T.N., Japan, 1960

Quisp Cosmiclouder Space Gun, plastic, 4¾ x 7½ in., Quaker Cereal, U.S.A. 1960s

Stingray, die-cast metal, 5½ x 7¼ in., Lone Star, England late 1960s

Space Rifle, lithographed tin, 2¾ x 11¾ in., maker unknown, England 1960s

Atomic Orbetor-X, plastic, 5½ x 11½ in., Gherzi, Italy 1960s

atomic orbetor-x®

Atomic Orbetor-X, box, 1¾ x 9 x 11½ in., Gherzi, Italy 1960s
Battle in Outer Space, movie poster, 16½ x 10¾ in., Columbia Pictures, U.S.A. 1960
Super Sonic Gun, box, 2 x 5 x 9½ in., Daiya, Japan 1960s

SPACE SUPER JET GUN
X-35
PAT. NO~
FRICTION POWERED WITH SPARKING

ATOMIC PISTOL
WITH SPARKS
Atomic
TRADE T.N MARK

TOY RAY GUN SOURCES

Website

Metcalf, Eugene W. *Toy Ray Guns.* http://www.toyraygun.com. Presents images of hundreds of toy ray guns and related items like holsters, space helmets, and space suits. Explores the aesthetic meaning, history, and cultural significance of these toys. A forum for interactive discussion and information exchange on the topic of toy ray guns.

Books

Cross, Gary. *Kids Stuff: Toys and the Changing World of American Childhood.* Cambridge: Harvard University Press, 1997. A fascinating social history of toys and their relationship to changing conceptions of childhood. Particularly interesting information on space toys and Buck Rogers.

Hake, Ted. *Hake's Price Guide to Character Toy Premiums*, Timonium, MD: Gemstone Publishing, Inc. 1996. Includes ray gun premiums in a number of sections. See particularly the sections on Buck Rogers, Captain Video, Flash Gordon, Space Patrol, and Tom Corbett Space Cadet.

Kitahara, Teruhisa. *Yesterdays Toys: Robots, Space Ships, and Monsters.* San Francisco: Chronicle Books, 1989. Includes six pages of color photographs of toy ray guns and their boxes.

Lesser, Robert. *A Celebration of Comic Art and Memorabilia.* New York: Hawthorn Books, 1975. A beautifully illustrated history and production list of great comic book and media characters from the late 19th century through the 1950s. The best information on Buck Rogers available.

Payton, Crystal and Leland. *Space Toys: A Collector's Guide to Science Fiction and Astronautical Toys.* Sedalia, Missouri: Collector's Compass. 1982. An early book on space toys. Includes a section on space guns.

Sansweet, Stephen J. *Science Fiction Toys and Models, Vol 1.* New York: Star Log Press. 1980.The first book on space toys. Includes many types of toys including some great illustrations of space guns.

Schneider, Stuart. *Collecting the Space Race.* Atglen, PA: Schiffer Publishing Lt. 1993. A complete guide to collecting space-related artifacts. One of the many sections focuses on ray guns.

Singer, Leslie. *Zap: Ray Gun Classics.* San Francisco: Chronicle Books. 1991. The first book on ray guns. Beautifully illustrated. Includes toys from the 1930s through the present.

LENDERS

Every attempt has been made to secure proper credit information on the images used in this book. However, it was not always possible to locate the original sources of ownership. We apologize for any oversights. The numbers listed below refer to the page numbers and position of the item.

Ray Amati 8, 9, 10, 15, 16, 17, 18 bottom left, 18–9, 20, 21, 23, 35 (badges)

David Greeman 74, 100

Dennis Merritt 33, 62 left, 62 right, 63 left, 64 top

Barbara Moran 68 left, 69 right, 84

Michael Schneider 65, 68 right, 69 left, 70, 76, 77, 78, 78–9, 79, 102 left, 102 right

Richard Thomas 38, 56–7, 64 bottom, 67, 75, 80, 80–1, 81, 89 right

Private Collection 11, 12, 13, 14, 18 top left, 19 left, 19 right, 22, 24, 25, 26, 26–7, 27, 28, 29, 30, 31, 32, 34 left, 34 right, 35 center, 36, 37, 39, 40, 41, 42, 43, 44, 45, 46 left, 46 right, 47, 48, 48–9, 49, 50 top left, 50 bottom left, 50 right, 51 left, 51 right, 52, 53, 54 left, 54 right, 55 left, 55 right, 56, 57, 58, 58–9, 59, 60, 60–1, 61, 63 right, 66, 71 left, 71 right, 72, 73, 82, 83, 85, 86, 87, 88 left, 88 right, 89 left, 90 left, 90 right, 91, 92 top left, 92 bottom left, 92 right, 93, 94, 94–5, 95, 96, 96–7, 97, 98, 98–9, 99, 100–1, 101, 103, 104, 105, 106, 107 left, 107 right, 108 109

Eugene W. Metcalf is Professor of Interdisciplinary Studies at Miami University in Ohio. A renowned scholar in the fields of American art and material culture, he has written and lectured extensively on folk, self-taught, and vernacular art. His authored works include seminal writings on the politics of African-American art, the social meaning of American folk art collecting, and the myth of the Self-Taught artist. He is co-editor of the major critical volume *The Artist Outsider: Creativity and the Boundaries of Culture.* Metcalf is also an avid collector of toy ray guns and the creator of an internationally acclaimed website devoted to ray guns and their role in the popular imagining of outer space.

As co-owner of the Ricco/Maresca Gallery in New York City, Frank Maresca is among America's most distinguished collectors and dealers of Outsider and Self-Taught art. He has co-authored several books published by Alfred A. Knopf, among them: *A Certain Style: The Art of the Plastic Handbag*, with Robert Gottlieb, *Bill Traylor: His Art, His Life, American Primitive, American Self-Taught: Drawings and Paintings by Outsider Artists*, and *William Hawkins: Paintings*, all co-authored with Roger Ricco. Maresca is also well known as a fashion photographer, and his work has appeared in *Vogue*, *Harper's Bazaar*, and *Town and Country*.

Charles Bechtold's photographs have been the highlight of numerous fine art books published by Alfred A. Knopf, among them *Bill Traylor: His Art, His Life, American Self-Taught: Drawings and Paintings by Outsider Artists*, and *William Hawkins: Paintings.* He was also a contributing photographer in the book *Passionate Visions of the American South.* His photographs also grace the pages of *Bill Traylor: Observing Life*, and *Charles A.A. Dellschau 1830–1923*, both produced by Ricco/Maresca Gallery. Bechtold lives in New Jersey and is a graduate of the School of Visual Arts in New York City.

ACKNOWLEDGMENTS

This book was written and compiled with the help of many friends. Leslie Singer shared his ray gun knowledge and enthusiasm in countless phone calls and E-mail messages. Ray Amati helped organize the "Buck Rogers" material in this book and loaned many of the toys presented in it. David Greeman, Dennis Merritt, Barbara Moran, Michael Schneider, and Richard Thomas generously loaned toys to be photographed. George Newcomb, of Plymouth Rock Toy Company, caught factual errors in the text and checked the dates of manufacture and maker's names for the toy guns presented here. Leonard Nimoy graciously shared a personal experience. Finally, Joanne Cubbs carefully edited the text of this book, giving it a "zap" it certainly would have lacked otherwise. Thank you.

Fotofolio, Inc.
561 Broadway, New York, New York 10012
Fotofolio: Martin Bondell, Juliette Galant, Ron Schick, Cindy Williamson, Justine Keefe
Printed in Korea
Library of Congress Catalog Card Number: 99-64972
ISBN: 1-58418-004-8 (hardcover)